GLOBAL MARKET BRIEFINGS

Albania's Business Environment

Consultant Editor:
Alica Henson

GMB

Publishers' note

Every possible effort has been made to ensure that the information contained in this publication is accurate at the time of going to press and neither the publishers nor any of the authors, editors, contributors or sponsors can accept responsibility for any errors or omissions, however caused. No responsibility for loss or damage occasioned to any person acting, or refraining from action, as a result of the material in this publication can be accepted by the editors, the authors, the publisher or any of the contributors or sponsors.

GMB Publishing Ltd and its authors, editors, contributors, partners, sponsors or endorsing bodies make no warranty, express or implied, concerning the information, and expressly disclaim all warranties.

The views expressed in the research materials and publications herein are those of the individual authors or contributors identified as the originators of each specific piece of research or publication and are not necessarily those of GMB Publishing Ltd or of any of the other authors, contributors, partners, sponsors or endorsing bodies. Views expressed within GMB Research or within GMB Publishing's print publications do not constitute legal advice or opinion and readers should where relevant seek appropriate legal advice.

Users and readers of this publication may copy or download portions of the material herein for personal use, and may include portions of this material in internal reports and/or reports to customers, and on an occasional and infrequent basis individual articles from the material, provided that such articles (or portions of articles) are attributed to this publication by name, the individual contributor of the portion used and GMB Publishing Ltd.

Users and readers of this publication shall not reproduce, distribute, display, sell, publish, broadcast, repurpose, or circulate the material to any third party, or create new collective works for resale or for redistribution to servers or lists, or reuse any copyrighted component of this work in other works, without the prior written permission of GMB Publishing Ltd.

GMB Publishing Ltd.
Hereford House
23-24 Smithfield Street
London EC1A 9LF
United Kingdom
www.globalmarketbriefings.com

525 South 4th Street, #241
Philadelphia, PA 19147
United States of America

First published in 2009 by GMB Publishing Ltd.

© GMB Publishing Ltd. and contributors

ISBN-13 978-1-84673-084-9
E-ISBN-13 978-1-84673-085-6

British Library Cataloguing in Publication Data
A CIP record for this book is available from the British Library

Library of Congress Cataloguing-in Publication Data

Typeset by David Lewis XML Associates Ltd.

Contents

Foreword

It is not infrequent to meet people who have little knowledge of Albania and what Albania looks like today. I wouldn't be surprised if many have an outdated perception of the situation and of the things we in Albania have achieved, how Albania looks today, and what it wants to achieve in the future. At a time when we are trying our best to promote and attract inward investment to Albania, I am particularly delighted to see ever increasing interest being generated right now in Albania's reality. It is becoming more and more visible in the Western media that Albania is today a very interesting and attractive destination. Opportunities do exist there and conditions are right and ripe to seriously consider moving in with investment. Albania, its institutions, its business community and the Albanian people are prepared and ready to work with the rest of the world.

This publication is another excellent opportunity to show that Albania has come a long way in its transformation. It provides a realistic vision for its future, in particular with regard to how to include international businesses, and the Albanian diaspora, in that vision.

We are glad to note an ever greater appreciation of our general efforts, progress and commitment in moving ahead with reforms, change and development in the country. The World Bank's *Doing Business 2008 Report*, which ranks Albania 86th out of 181 countries (up from 135th), also places it as the second top reformer globally with regard to business environment reforms implemented over the past year.

The Albanian authorities' commitment to sound macroeconomic and well-anchored structural reforms has been highlighted by the International Monetary Fund: "Thanks to generally prudent policies, Albania's economy largely passed a demanding test in 2007, despite challenges from a difficult external environment. Growth improved and inflation expectations remained low, notwithstanding a drought and rising food and energy prices. Prudent fiscal and monetary policies were key in this regard, while ongoing structural reform is reaping rewards from improved competitiveness."

The World Bank further commented: "Albania's record since it embarked on its transition in the early 1990s has been impressive. The country has successfully built the foundations of market-based economy, created democratic institutions and gradually built capacity in the public administration to cope with political and economic transformation. These efforts have resulted in a track record of macroeconomic stability, as well as achievement of the fastest rates of GDP growth in South Eastern Europe."

Our objectives are clear, our plans are clear, our determination is there. In these efforts we are not asking for any commitment. We are actually sharing our commitment to the targets we have set ourselves and to our resolve. Ingenuity will be displayed and imagination evoked from a large number of competent people, diligent companies and very business-minded individuals in Albania to ensure that we will make it. We are aware also that international cooperation, in particular from developed countries, strong economies and international financial institutions, will be required as we move ahead.

We are hopeful that, given the highly improved, secure, normal and attractive environment, this cooperation will not be lacking and foreign investors will be rewarded by coming to invest in Albania.

Zef Mazi
Ambassador of Albania to the United Kingdom of Great Britain and Northern Ireland and to the Republic of Ireland

Foreword

Albania is situated in the south-western coast of the South East Europe region with a population of 3.8 million. The country began its transitional phase from 1991, the year that marked the opening of the country to the outside world and the lifting of the ban on foreign capital and private initiative. Since that time, the country has made significant progress in completing the legislative framework by introducing modern and sophisticated laws, with a particular focus on laws and regulations that improve the business climate. Albania is working hard on reforms that are aimed at the strengthening of law enforcement. Such attitude has been seen as a guaranty for the safety and fairness in doing business in Albania—so much so that the country was recently given a rating of "B1" by Moody's, which is more or less similar to that of Croatia, Bulgaria, Ukraine, Indonesia and Jamaica.

Albania is a member of the International Bank for Reconstruction and Development (IBRD), European Bank for Reconstruction and Development (EBRD), World Trade Organization (WTO), etc., and is signatory of several regional and bilateral treaties on investment protection and economic cooperation and some 30 double tax treaties. Albania has preferential regimes with the United States, Australia, New Zealand, Switzerland, Norway, Russia, Japan and Canada and has also signed a Free Trade Agreement with Turkey.

Some factors that have made the country attractive are the steady GDP growth rate, stable currency, a strong banking sector, and the notable foreign language proficiency of the young workforce, many of whom are well educated, are accustomed to international best practices and possess excellent language skills.

The fantastic location in the Balkans has made Albania increasingly be seen as a springboard for expanding investment opportunities to the wider regional market. It has also become increasingly attractive for tourism, with its impressive coast being referred to as the last untouched frontier of Europe.

Key sectors include tourism, real estate, oil, energy, cement, agriculture and the food processing industry, mining, infrastructure and information and communication technology.

The country is fully committed to modernizing the economy and the information society, as these are conditions necessary to move ahead with the process of European Union (EU) integration, which has already been initiated by the signing of the Stabilization and Association Agreement (SAA) in 2006. In addition, Albania is putting tremendous efforts into joining

NATO, and the country received a formal invitation to enter into accession negotiations following the latest summit in Bucharest in April 2008.

Within this ambit, Albania is improving the business climate by introducing anti-corruption programmes in the business registration and licensing process and also by implementing a profound legal and judicial reform and by increasing transparency in the public procurement and concession bidding procedures. The government is making steps forward to introducing e-commerce and e-procurement and has ambitious programmes for internet services, with a view to introducing them in all schools.

The government recently introduced a flat tax rate of 10 per cent on any income as of January 2008 and also abolished customs duties on almost all its car imports in line with WTO commitments; duties on car imports from the EU have also abolished under the SAA, but some environmental taxes on old cars have been increased.

Investors continue to show an increased interest in the country's energy sector through the building and operation of hydropower plants on a concession basis. Recently, important regional energy players have been contracted for four significant hydropower plants worth in total €1.5 billion.

Other recent significant investments are the construction of two cement plants in the vicinity of Tirana, valued at €170 million and €250 million, respectively.

To conclude, Albanians are very friendly and welcome all foreigners, be it for pleasure or business.

Përparim Kalo
Founding and Managing Partner, Kalo & Associates

About the Contributors

Deloitte was established in Albania in 1996 and is regarded as the leading professional services firm in the country. Deloitte Albania employs over 40 people and is continuously expanding and developing. The firm has achieved remarkable results within the short period of its presence in Albania, providing Audit and Advisory, Tax, Legal, Consulting, Accounting and Financial Advisory Services to many of Albania's leading companies.

Dawn Connolly, Senior Manager – International Tax Services, joined Deloitte Albania in June 2008, with over five years' experience advising multinational clients on international tax planning matters in Silicon Valley as well as two years in Luxembourg. Dawn is a CPA in the State of Maryland and an attorney-at-law (State of California), having earned a Juris Doctorate from the University of California – Hastings College of the Law, as well as Baccalaureates in Business and Economics from the University of Maryland. Ms Connolly has also studied European tax law with the LLM program at Maastricht University (Netherlands) as well as US tax law with Golden Gate University's LLM program in San Francisco.

Nuriona Sokoli is a manager in the Audit Department of Deloitte Albania. Ms Sokoli is a graduate of Tirana University with a BA in Finance and Banking and she is also an ACCA member. She is a certified accountant in Kosova and is registered as an independent account in the IEKA list. She is an active member of Financial Services Group of Deloitte Central Europe. Ms Sokoli has three years' extensive experience with the audit department, involved mainly in audit of financial institutions, manufacturing sector, public sector, and other project financed from other international organizations. She joined the audit practice after an extensive experience in the tax department of Deloitte Albania and she has gained significant experience in tax advice and limited tax audit. She has a very good understanding of Albanian fiscal law and local accounting standards. She speaks fluent English, Italian and French.

Dorina Tila, Consultant – International Tax Services, joined Deloitte Albania in September 2008, with over two years' experience with consulting in efficient economic systems design. She has earned a B.S. in Economics from University of La Verne and a PhD in Experimental Economics and Industrial Organization from George Mason University, Virginia.

The largest law firm in Albania with over 30 lawyers, **Kalo & Associates** was originally established and founded by Përparim Kalo in 1994. The firm rapidly developed into a prominent and successful practice offering high quality, efficient, and cost-effective legal services. Now with two offices, one in Tirana and the second in Prishtina, Kalo & Associates has six partners.

The firm has a team of quality lawyers that are highly trained, many of whom hold post-graduate qualifications with some having gained their qualifications outside of Albania. All lawyers are known to have excellent relations with their clients and are adept in providing the right solution for the client in resolving the legal problems they face. The close team network means that all lawyers are able to draw upon the expertise of others in the firm to help provide a complete, comprehensive service and anticipate and defuse any potential legal problems.

The firm offers legal services in all core areas of commercial and corporate law for foreign and multinational companies, many of which are Fortune 500.

The primary areas of practice are:

- Corporate (JVs/M&A)
- Concessions/PPPS/Infrastructure Projects
- Government Contracts
- Energy/Gas/Petroleum/Mining/Utilities
- Competition (Merger Control)
- Banking
- Factoring/Financial Leasing
- Project Financing
- Securities/Investment Funds
- Insurance
- Agency/Distributorship/Franchising
- International Sales of Goods/Cross-Border

- Product Liability
- IP
- ICT/Telecommunications
- E-contracts
- Media
- Tax/Taxation
- Tax/Corporate Restructuring
- Bankruptcy/Insolvency/Liquidation
- Employment/Employment Benefits
- Commercial Arbitration/Litigation/ Mediation
- Real Estate
- Planning /Construction/Environment Agreements

The firm is active in legislative development, having provided input on the new corporate and municipal bonds law, collective investment funds and pension funds law; and has in the past advised on the drafting of financial leasing, insurance, and the concession law.

One London based legal publisher (IFLR1000) describes the firm as having *"a practice that is consistent with what you would expect from a top Washington law firm"*. Another publisher quotes a client who has expressed the confidence in the firm's unshakeable integrity by saying: *"this thoroughly reputable group always leaves you completely satisfied"*.

Përparim Kalo is the Founding and Managing Partner of Kalo & Associates. Mr Kalo established his private practice in 1994. Previous to this, he was in-house counsel for the Albanian Insurance Institute (INSIG) from 1993 to 1994; he was Head of the Department for the Land Registry and Notaries in the Ministry of Justice (1990-1992) and worked in the Ministry of Justice's Department of International Affairs. Mr Kalo has been a member of the American Chamber of Commerce since 2005; he was Commissioner of the Albanian Securities Commission in 2005 and Overseer at INSIG from 1999 to 2000. He has been a member of the Tirana Bar Association and the Albanian Country Representative of the International Bar Association since 1994. He was also a Founding and Board Member of the Albanian Centre for Dispute Resolution from 1995 to 2000. Mr Kalo speaks Albanian, English and Italian.

Sophia Darling is a recently appointed Partner of the firm. She is a UK qualified solicitor, having practised in the UK as a solicitor in a range of areas and focused her training on commercial work. Her focus now is particularly in the fields of commercial transactions, project financing and IP. She has developed a very good working knowledge of the legal system in Albania and combining this successfully with the extensive legal skills acquired through practising in England she offers a valuable service to all clients.

Jona Bica is Head of the Banking and Finance Department. She graduated with a BA Honours in Legal Studies in 2006 from Tirana University. Having previously come from a media background, she has been working at Kalo & Associates for approximately three years. During the last two years, she has been exposed to many areas of the legal sector and although she has focused on the banking and finance sector she has had the opportunity to carry out work also within the corporate department, revising and drafting commercial contracts, and also working as legal adviser performing M&A legal works. She speaks Albanian, English, German and Italian.

Alessandro Boscaino, Associate of the Infrastructure Department, began his career at the Hon. Alberto Simeone Law Firm in Italy where he assisted with litigation in the local and appellate courts involving a wide range of civil law matters and some criminal cases. Subsequently at the Furlan Law Firm he worked on cases involving commercial and financial disputes and private international law. During his time in the United States he joined a large DC law firm where he worked on a project regarding a government investigation on foreign and corporate bribes. Since joining Kalo & Associates in Tirana in May 2007, he has been assigned to various projects in the energy sector.

Shirli Gorenca is an Associate in the Intellectual Property and International Contracts Department. She has been working at Kalo & Associates for one-and-a-half years and has recently joined this department. She graduated with a BA Honours in Legal Studies in 2007 from Tirana University. Since joining Kalo & Associates, she spent time both within the Banking and Property Departments drafting banking contracts, sale contracts, lease contracts, etc. She speaks Albanian, English and Italian.

Emel Haxhillari, Associate, Department of Tax/Employment, graduated from the faculty of law at the South East European University in Tetovo, Macedonia (having focused on administrative and tax law). She has further completed a postgraduate degree in European Studies at the University of Tirana. Emel has previously worked for the Central Election Commission and now works with the firm within the tax and employment department. She is fluent in Albanian, English and Italian.

Eni Kalo is an Associate in the IP and ICT Department. She completed a Masters Degree in IP Law at Strasbourg University ("Robert Schuman"). Eni also completed her law degree at the same prestigious university in Strasbourg. She provides a very strong knowledge of both EU practice and legal procedures that is of invaluable benefit both to the firm and clients. Her main focus is towards IP, EU law and commercial contracts. Eni is fluent in Albanian, French, English and Italian.

Florian Piperi is a Senior Associate and Head of the Litigation and Arbitration Department. He is widely recognized as one of the leading lawyers in the enforcement of defaulted bank loans in Albania. His extensive first-hand experience in areas of secured financed loans, finance transactions and contract enforcement has placed him in the forefront of many of the country's most important enforcement and litigation matters. Mr Piperi's practice focuses primarily on litigations, enforcement and contracts. He is also a member of the Albanian Mediator Association. He speaks Albanian, English and Italian.

Anisa Rrumbullaku is Head of Corporate and Business Licensing. Ms Rrumbullaku has been working with Kalo & Associates for over three years. Her experience encompasses legal advice on local corporate issues, business restructurings and infrastructure projects related to water, energy, mining, etc. for prominent international companies such as Occidental Petroleum, ENEL, EVN, HOCHTIEF AirPort, etc. She holds an LLM (cum laude) in Business and Trade Law and her practice focus is on projects awarded to the clients through public tenders, ie. drafting of due diligence reports, concession and PPP agreements and other government contracts, preparation of incorporation and registration documents and any other corporate related matters.

Ardjana Shehi, Head of Tax and Employment Department at Kalo & Associates, is a member of the Albanian Bar Association and holds an MBA degree. Ms Shehi has extensive experience—more than 18 years—in commercial law and, in particular, contract law, telecommunication, procurement and joint ventures. She now focuses particularly on the fields of tax, employment and bankruptcy. She has been a trainer in various training activities organized in Albania (including training on bankruptcy law). She is also a co-author of the *Teaching Manual for Judges on Bankruptcy*, a publication of School of Magistrates in Albania.

Zamira Xhaferri, Head of the Commercial Property Department, previously worked for the Office of the Albanian Prime Minister providing legal expertise to the Prime Minister together with international experts from the Institute for Liberty and Democracy under the "Transition to Rule of Law and an Inclusive Market Economy in Albania" project aimed at improving acquisition and economic use of property rights. The project focused on reform of the legal and institutional framework with respect to property rights, urban planning/town planning issues, restitution and compensation of properties, registration of immovable properties, and legalization of informal immovable properties. Ms Xhaferri has also been working for the OSCE in Albania as National Legal Expert, providing along with international experts legal expertise to the government of Albania.

Ard Kelmendi, FX & Commodities Specialist at Bloomberg, was born in Prishtina, Kosovo. He has lived in the UK for over 10 years, held internships at BBC World, and studied German at University College London.

Raiffeisen Bank Albania is the largest bank in Albania with assets of €2 billion, 100 branches and over 1,400 employees. Raiffeisen International purchased the Savings Bank of Albania in April 2004, and over the last three years the bank has transformed into a full service bank providing the full product range to all sectors of the country. Raiffeisen Bank of Albania occupies the number one position on all key market share measures and reported a profit of just under €40 million for 2006.

Robert Wright is Board Member for Retail Banking for Raiffeisen Bank Albania, and has 20 years of international retail banking experience. He started his banking career with HSBC in the UK and also worked for the Bank of Scotland and Abbey National where he was retail banking director. In 2000, he moved to a senior management position with Al Rajhi Bank, the largest bank in Saudi Arabia before moving to Raiffeisen Bank Albania in 2004.

Part One

Background to the Market

1.1

Political Background

Ard Kelmendi

Brief history of transition

Albania was the last country to emerge from the communist dictatorship in South Eastern Europe. It was also the poorest economically with a suppressed society whose members were not permitted to travel abroad. The fall of communism opened the doors to democracy; it led to a pluralist party system and a market economy, ideas which were completely alien to most Albanian politicians and leaders who were severely indoctrinated by the communist propaganda and ideology which had led to the execution and imprisonment of many regime opponents. This inability or lack of experience to adapt to a new era created an uneasy political atmosphere. Modern Albanian politics have been marred by party feuds, lack of inter-party cooperation and weak governments. These features have deprived the country of a strong leadership that can tackle urgent issues such as chronic power shortages, corruption, organized crime, etc. However, recent developments have shown an improved picture. The Albanian leadership has shown its commitment to deal with human trafficking, and the current government has taken concrete measures against it. Moreover, the current government has led the country into NATO, which it considers to be one of the greatest steps towards western integration.

Albania declared independence from the Ottoman Empire in 1912 and enjoyed a brief period of self-rule in the 15th century. Like most of the countries in South Eastern Europe, Albania's political framework has been a mishmash of systems. After its creation, the country became a principality under German Prince William of Wied (1914) who managed to rule the country for a mere six months due to internal strife and Greek occupation of the south. His exile created a political vacuum as the principality was left without a crown, although the Prince insisted continuously that he would return.

In the early 1920s Albania become a republic and in September 1928 the Albanian crown was claimed by Ahmet Zogu, who had governed the country as president and now declared himself King of the Albanians and transformed the country into a monarchy.

After the Italian occupation of the country in 1939, Albania ceased to function as an independent state and was governed as a protectorate of the Kingdom of Italy under Victor Emmanuel III. It then finally became a socialist republic in 1945, when the communists (led by paranoid despot Enver Hoxha) took over. Albania was kept firmly under communist control until March 1992, when the opposition, spearheaded by the Democratic Party under the leadership of Sali Berisha, won the first general elections since the fall of the red regime.

The brutal communist establishment followed strict isolationist policies which prohibited any form of international contact and were aimed at creating a centralized self-sufficient economy. Externally, their unwavering belief in Stalinist and Marxist-Leninist ideologies created irreparable damage to Soviet-Albanian and Sino-Albanian relations, and left the country in a political quagmire, separated from both the East and the West. Soviet leader Nikita Khrushchev had criticized Stalin's policies and China had agreed to relax hostilities with the United States, the main antagonist of the communist world. Hoxha deemed their actions as treacherous to the communist cause and proclaimed Albania as the only truly socialist state in the world.

Internally, the authorities attempted to win the loyalty of the masses by sponsoring a dogmatic educational system, abolishing religious practices (Albania officially became an atheist state in 1967, after a Chinese-style cultural revolution), encouraging relentless economic and political propaganda all of which were backed up by the vicious and fearful secret police agency, the Sigurimi. Towards the end of the 1980s, the failing economic policies had created social havoc and poverty across the country. This combined with political isolation proved to be a major hindrance to the development of Albania during its transitional period in the 1990s.

After Sali Berisha won the first free elections in 1992, he immediately pushed for reforms by embracing free market policies, endorsing trade liberalization and initiating the privatization of state held properties. Transforming an essentially barter economy into an open market one was particularly troublesome, as it desperately required a modern fiscal system and the establishment of a legal framework for business. On the other hand, social tensions fuelled by poverty and lack of prospects led to mass migration of Albanians particularly to neighbouring Greece and Italy. Unemployment rates increased as state enterprises could no longer compete with imported goods, and industrial and agricultural production shrank to the lowest levels.

On the international political platform, Berisha's administration placed the country firmly into a pro-western path by declaring their ambition to join the European Union (EU) and NATO. Diplomatic relations with the West were re-established, starting with the United States and the United Kingdom in 1991, although the West German Embassy was opened as far back as 1987 in Tirana. Albania became a member state of the Organization for Security and Cooperation in Europe (OSCE) in 1991, and joined the

North Atlantic Cooperation Council in 1992. In 1995, Albania was accepted in the Council of the European Union, and in September 1996, the Albanian parliament, Kuvendi, agreed to dispatch a military contingent to Bosnia to take part in the peace-keeping mission there.

However, Berisha's administration and his leadership were perceived to be extremely oppressive and corrupt given their highly uncompromising and irreconcilable approach towards the opposition led by former communists, who re-branded themselves under the Socialist Party of Albania. The last communist president, Ramiz Alia, was imprisoned after being accused of political corruption in 1993, followed by the immediate captivity of the Socialist Party leader, Fatos Nano. A year later, a district court in Tirana issued an arrest warrant under the pretext of embezzlement for Nexhmije Hixha, the wife of the late dictator Enver Hoxha. Such actions were regarded as acts of personal vengeance by members of the Democratic Party who had suffered enormously in communist jails.

Critically, these acts of retribution and the emergence of an arguably oppressive atmosphere under Berisha, together with a consistent decline in the living standards, seriously weakened poplar support for the Democrats, so much so that in 1994 the government lost a national referendum to amend the constitution.

The May 1996 election further weakened the position of the democrats after they claimed 90 per cent of the parliamentary seats. This election was denounced by national and international observers who quoted regular occurrences of intimidation, manipulation of the electoral commission and violence in the voting process. Calls by the Socialist Party to annul the election were completely ignored by the government.

The breaking point came in December 1996, when numerous Ponzi schemes went bankrupt, which nearly drove the country into an open civil war. Hundreds of thousands of Albanians had invested in dubious investment schemes which promised high returns in a very short period of time. Many Albanians had sold their houses, land and cattle in the hopes that they would receive huge payouts and become rich very quickly. Unfortunately, these investment plans were doomed from the start due to the sheer magnitude of interest rates offered to investors out of a rapidly shrinking pool of money. People demanded answers about the sudden financial collapse and held the government directly responsible for allowing the development of such fraudulent schemes.

By March 1997, Albania was in chaos as horrific civil unrest ensued, engulfing all parts of the country. Within this anarchy, Leka I (son of the late King Zog) attempted to take the throne but a referendum on the restoration of monarchy failed. The government was forced to resign and an interim government led by the Socialist Party took control. New elections in June 1997 reaffirmed the Socialists as the new governing force with Fatos Nano as the premier.

The socialists ruled the country until July 2005. Their key priorities were to secure absolute control in all parts of the country after a near civil war, restore public confidence in governmental institutions, control the spiralling inflation and deal with the looming Kosovan crisis in the north. At the same time they had to deal with an uncooperative opposition which continuously boycotted parliament. By 1998, inflation was halved to 20 per cent and it has continued to fall since then; moreover the government successfully managed to neutralize the insurgents in the south and take overall control. However, the import-export imbalance continued to rely heavily on remittances from Albanians living abroad and this still remains an outstanding feature of the Albanian economy.

Political unrests remained clear features of the day-to-day life. The September 1998 assassination of a Democratic Party activist led to violent protests across the country which eventually forced Fatos Nano to resign. He was replaced by a younger charismatic socialist, Pandeli Majko, who faced the enormous challenge of dealing with thousands of incoming Kosovan refugees who were being forced out of their homes. The last war of Yugoslavia created a rare solidarity among the main Albanian parties who condemned the Serbian clampdown on their cousins in Kosovo. However, Majko's premiership was soon threatened after an internal election in the Socialist Party which saw the emergence of Ilir Meta as its new leader which also made him the new prime minister. At the age of 30, Meta became Europe's youngest prime minister and he would lead the Socialist Party to another electoral victory in 2001.

Meta's emergence as a new leader of the Socialist Party created an ever-widening rift between him and the party chairman, Fatos Nano. Ideological differences and Meta's repeated calls for reform within the party ignited irreconcilable differences between the two. Nano's strong influence in the party was confirmed when he demanded the resignation of two ministers in Meta's cabinet who obeyed without any objections. In January 2002, Meta resigned after failing to ease the party feuds and Majko became prime minister again. In the same year, the Royal Family returned from exile and both parties agreed on electing Alfred Moisiu as the republic's president. In a final governmental reshuffle, the Socialist Party agreed to merge the roles of premiership and party chairman, thus allowing Fatos Nano to become prime minister again.

Current government

The current government is a centre-right coalition led by former President Sali Berisha's Democratic Party (PD) and parties such as the Republican Party, the Christian Democratic Party, etc. The coalition enjoys a comfortable majority although it needed opposition support to elect Bamir Topi as president in July 2007. The PD has also managed to re-merge with a splinter group that had previously separated from its main body. The Socialist Party remains the strongest force in the opposition.

In November 2008, parliament passed a new electoral code based on a European model after another rare consensus between the PD and the Socialist Party. Many hope that this new code will help fix Albania's vote irregularities which have so far dominated every single election. However, the new electoral regulation has not been accepted by smaller parties, particularly the Movement for Socialist Integration, which is led by the former Prime Minister Ilir Meta, citing their deliberate exclusion from the election committee under the new code. Their fierce protests included a hunger strike in the national parliament which the cabinet has done little to resolve.

NATO and EU accession

Albania was invited to join NATO at the Bucharest Summit in April 2008, seen by many as a reward for the current leadership's reforms in the army. This has firmly aligned Albania's military with the West and perhaps shows that a degree of political stability has finally reached this corner of Europe. Albania signed the Stabilization and Association Agreement with the EU thereby completing one of the key steps towards full EU membership. This process is, however, going to be a long one as major reforms are needed to tackle corruption and organized crime, as well as other problems facing Albanian society. Albania needs to convince the world that it can organize fair and stable elections; despite numerous measures by the government, human trafficking and other forms of organized crime continue to be serious obstacles; the judiciary is still prone to bribery, and many judgments have been proven to be biased. Lastly, property laws need to be strengthened and illegal property ownership needs to be addressed if the country intends to develop a competing tourist industry.

1.2

Economic Background

Ard Kelmendi

History and nature of transition

Albania's transition into the market economy was an uphill struggle compared to neighbouring countries. Albania was poorer, and the harsh communist dictatorship, which had controlled the country since the Second World War, had produced a chaotic and backward economy. After the regime change, initial signs were positive; however, lack of experience, corruption and organized crime continued to undermine the country's performance, so much so that in 1997 Albania became victim to a bitter internal struggle. Recently Albania has enjoyed a comfortable economic growth, the tourist and construction industries are booming, the road infrastructure and financial services have seen major improvement, and in August 2008, inflation sat comfortably at 2.5 per cent year-on-year. Moreover Albania signed the Stabilization and Association Agreement (SAA) with the European Union (EU) in June 2006, and in April 2008 received an invitation to join NATO. However, there is still major room for improvement in combating corruption, resolving the property rights question, improving power supplies and eradicating human trafficking and drug smuggling, which continue to project a less than positive image of this small European country.

In March 1992, Albania emerged from one of the most ruthless communist dictatorships in Europe. It had been brutally ruled for four decades by the paranoid and staunchly Stalinist despot, Enver Hoxha, who effectively isolated the country from the rest of the world, with any form of external contact punishable by death. The post-war communist regime cited historic and recent invasions of the country to justify their xenophobic and fearful political strategy.

In a similar way to other countries within the Soviet Bloc, the communists in Albania believed in a centralized planned economy and prioritized nationalization of private land, and the development of agriculture and heavy industry to ensure an egalitarian society. These measures immediately transformed the face of the country and for the first time for many years, the majority peasant population of Albania enjoyed a higher standard of living. Illiteracy rates dropped and thanks to the communists encouraging a pro-family ideology, the Albanian population rose from 1.2 million in 1950 to 3.3 million in 1990.

As a communist state, though, Albania could not gain access to International Monetary Fund (IMF) or World Bank funding and thus relied heavily on Soviet and Chinese assistance. And even their support was cut off after Hoxha voiced his strong criticism of Soviet Premier Nikita Khrushchev's de-Stalinization policies in 1961, which relaxed restrictions on private plots, and after China decided to re-emerge from isolation by normalizing relations with the United States in the 1970s. Albania was thus alienated from both East and West, and adopted a "go-it-alone" policy which left the economy completely sealed off from other world markets. The regime (led by Ramiz Alia after Hoxha's death in 1985) insisted on the concept of autarky or economic self-reliance as the answer to the country's development. Alas, industrial and agricultural production was constrained by the mismanagement and inefficiency that epitomized communist systems elsewhere. Eventually, when Albania did open up to the world, national self-sufficiency proved to be a catastrophic failure, as most industrial enterprises could not compete against imported goods and also because this concept provided no clear guide to international competitive costs.

The latter part of the 1980s continued to witness a decline in Albania's economy. State-controlled companies were operating under a permanent shadow of deficient resources, production reached its lowest levels, and agricultural cooperatives could no longer afford to pay their employees. As a result, the central government in Tirana introduced food rationing to deal with the crisis.

The wind of change that had encapsulated the Soviet Bloc finally reached Albania and the crippled government bowed to external and internal pressure for change. Restrictions on foreign travel were lifted, the state withdrew its control from some retail prices, citizens were no longer forbidden from owning private cars and the produce from private plots could be sold in the markets. However, these reforms proved to be belated and insufficient; moreover it showed the elite's unwillingness to yield power to the opposition group led by Sali Berisha, the leader of the Democratic Party of Albania (DPA). When Berisha's party did win the general elections in March 1992, Albania embarked on its transition path as the poorest and most rural country in Europe, with a predominantly barter economy and reliant on foreign food aid to feed its population.

Immediately after taking office, the democratically elected government pushed for energetic reforms to alleviate the economic deterioration and place the country firmly on course for a market economy. Crucially this included integrating a new fiscal system, lifting all restrictions on price movements and currency exchanges, setting up a legal system for the market and initiating the privatization of state-controlled enterprises. A noted achievement was the reduction of inflation to the second lowest in Central and Eastern Europe; 5 per cent in 1995, and 17 per cent in 1996. Furthermore, Albania became a member of the IMF, the World Bank and the European Bank of Reconstruction and Development (EBRD), which enabled the country to seek external funding.

However, by the end of 1995 it was clear that these measures manifested negative results. The liberalization of prices and foreign trade led to the irreversible collapse of domestic production, because the industry was losing domestic clients previously guaranteed under the planned economy. Furthermore, the state simply could not safeguard industrial production against the highly competitive nature of foreign trade. In addition, agricultural output fell under the combined effect of a severe drought and the chaotic break-up of collective farms, which dipped the country into poverty and forced many people to emigrate. Crucial to this looming crisis was the government's inability to tackle the stagnating financial sector, which gradually led to the emergence of an informal market, dominated by Ponzi schemes, whose eventual collapse would sink the country into a near civil war in 1997.

Fraudulent investment companies without any real assets promised high returns. These returns were paid to the first investors out of the funds received from those who invested later. The scheme was thus insolvent from the day it opened for business. Incredible interest rates were offered and at their peak, the nominal value of the Ponzi schemes' liabilities amounted to almost half of the country's GDP. When companies began to default towards the end of 1996, angry investors sought government compensation and directly blamed them for their losses. By March 1997, Albania was in chaos as horrific civil unrest ensued, engulfing all parts of the country. The government was forced to resign and an interim government led by the successors of the communist party (now re-branded the Socialist Party of Albania) took control.

Recent macroeconomic performance and outlook

The government now had to deal with rising inflation (42 per cent in 1997), a near collapse of the tax collection system, a sharp depreciation of the leke against the US dollar (down 40 per cent), falling remittances from abroad, a stark reduction of foreign aid and a slowdown in international trade. However, stability was quick to follow, owing to the prudent monetary and fiscal policies and increasing remittances from Albanians working abroad. The latter was and remains crucial in compensating the lack of lending from the banking sector, has helped to lower the export/import imbalance and has set the stage for the development of the construction industry. By 2001, financial contributions from abroad amounted to about 15 per cent of GDP and many analysts believe that this figure is a lot higher. Analysts also predict an eventual decline in remittances, which could have a significant impact on the Albanian economy, given its high GDP share. Remittances from abroad continued to increase from the year 2000 onwards, reaching $1.161 billion in 2005.

Table 1. Remittances by Albanians living abroad ($ million)

1996	1997	1998	1999	2000	2001	2002	2003	2004	2005
500	267	452	368	531	615	632	778	1,028	1,161

Source: Bank of Albania, Remittances: Albanian Experience, June 2006

Table 2. GDP growth ($ billion)

	1996	1997	1998	1999	2000	2001	2002	2003	2004	2005
GDP	3.36	2.375	2.768	3.49	3.709	4.114	4.505	5.859	7.549	8.38

Source: Bank of Albania, Remittances: Albanian Experience, June 2006

By 2001, inflation was down 3.5 per cent, and GDP grew to an impressive $4.114 billion from $3.49 billion in the previous year, and by 2005 it rose to $8.38 billion. The IMF expects 6 per cent growth in 2008. Exports doubled from $305 million in 2001 to $659 million in 2005, while imports also saw a vast increase from $1.332 billion in 2001 to $2.486 billion in 2005. There have been outstanding changes in the composition of GDP by sector, with services replacing agriculture at 58 per cent, which in 2001 was recorded at 51 per cent, mainly due to the development of the tourism sector. Industry has also seen an increase from 11.5 per cent in 2001 to 15 per cent in 2005, with the rest of the percentages shared between the construction and transport industries. In August 2008, nominal GDP stood at 1.0783 trillion Albanian leke (ALL) and the annual change in the consumer price index was 2.5 per cent, an increase of 0.6 per cent from the previous month. The trade balance remains negative at ALL –172,640 billion, with imports vastly exceeding exports at ALL 240.946 billion against ALL 68.306 billion and the 12-month treasury bill yielded at 8.15 per cent.

Sectoral profile

As indicated earlier, the sectoral composition of the GDP has seen tremendous change since 2001, and this process is still in progress. The influence of remittances from abroad on the nation's GDP could dwindle as a result of the rapid development of the tourism industry. This sector could most certainly be a vital tool in lifting the country out of poverty and the authorities have undertaken steps to promote the vastly unexplored Albanian Riviera. In 2006, the tourism industry amounted to 77 per cent of Albanian exports and gained €805 million that year alone. The number of foreign visitors to the country has been growing rapidly every year, recorded at 1.126 million in 2007. However, none of Albania's beaches meet Blue Flag criteria on water quality, environmental management, education and information, and there is no similarly recognized system of assessment of beaches. Moreover, several beaches along the Albanian coast are reported to be polluted as a result of inadequate sewage disposal and treatment.

The tourism industry, though, is seeing vast improvements due to ongoing and completed infrastructure projects. Many roads are being built along the coast and in the south of country, culminating with the monumental, but over-budget, Rreshen–Kalimash motorway (set to be completed in summer 2009), which links the coastal city of Durres with the northern city of Kukes, near the Kosovan border. Tirana International Airport has been modernized and port cities have also undergone major improvements. However, much remains to be done in the Albanian railway system, which currently does not operate any international passenger services.

There have also been some positive movements in resolving the country's endemic power shortages, which many believe is the main inhibitor of foreign investments. The Albanian government has recently accepted a bid of €102 million by the Czech power company CEZ for a 76 per cent stake in the national electricity operator OSSH. CEZ have promised to spend €586 million to upgrade the obsolete supply grids, which is badly needed in this sector. Additionally, the Austrian electricity company Verbund has signed a deal with the government to build a hydropower plant to increase energy capacity. However, for the moment, severe power shortages are a reality in most Albanian villages and small towns. Without a steady supply of energy, the development of the Albanian economy as a whole faces serious challenges to compete with other regional economies.

Industrial production is weak and the country's vast natural resources remain generally unexploited. In the 1980s, Albania was the world's third largest producer of chromium ore, but this has now dwindled considerably. The erratic supply of electricity, lack of foreign investment, decline in domestic demand and high maintenance cost have also hit the once thriving mining sector. There has, however, been a revival in oil reserves after the Canadian company Bankers Petroleum signed an agreement with the government for a 25-year licence to develop large oil reserves, which include the Patos Marinza oil field, the largest onshore oil field in continental Europe. The government has also announced plans to build four industrial parks in the country, which could facilitate the strengthening of industrial output.

1.3

Business Environment

Ard Kelmendi

Introduction

Albania became a member of the World Trade Organization (WTO) in September 2000. Since that time, the country has strived to implement the essential principles fostered by this institution, namely guaranteeing equal rights for both foreign and domestic companies and implementing transparent laws for the market.

Albania has made visible improvements in these fields, some of which have been clearly confirmed by the World Bank in the "Doing Business 2009" report. Bureaucracy and complex administrative procedures have been relaxed and a very liberal law which dictates company regulations was put in place as early as November 1992.

Internal and regional political instability has hindered the much needed progress in the development of a competitive business atmosphere, but now Albania has consolidated its position in the region and is emerging rapidly as one of the key economic players. Moody's Ba1 sovereign rating carries a stable outlook for the country which reflects this new power. Moreover, Albania offers a very versatile labour market, great prospects in the tourism and real estate industries and opportunities in the energy sector.

Nonetheless, the Albanian business environment is still riddled with a weak arbitrage and judicial system; and corruption continues to damage its much needed development, despite promising efforts by the current government to eradicate it.

In the World Bank's "Doing Business 2009", Albania is listed among the top 10 reformers globally (second only to Azerbaijan) during the 2007–2008 period and is currently ranked 86th, which is a +49 improvement from the previous year. It now takes eight days to set up a business in the country, compared to 15 in Greece. According to the report, Albania has made crucial progress in the investor protection index, which evaluates guidelines concerning self-dealings and personal gains from the illegal use of corporate assets. The country is ranked 14th in this category, compared to its former position of 168th.

Moreover, the country has also been praised in the "getting credit" category, ranked 12th globally, which is a key consideration in assessing risk and allocating credit more efficiently. In the "paying taxes" category, which determines the efficiency of the tax system and takes into consideration how business taxes are spent, despite reassuring commitments, Albania still lags behind other countries in the region. Overall, though, this report clearly reveals a positive change in the Albanian business climate and is a reassuring signal that the country is gradually laying the key foundations for the development of a sound economy.

However, much needs to be done to resolve the land reform and property rights question, particularly in coastal areas, which is preventing foreign companies from investing in the exquisite tourist and property sectors. The World Bank report has understandably lowered Albania's ranking in this category from 56th in 2008 down to 62nd for 2009. The so-called "land mafia" continues to operate illegal property trades on the Albanian coast said to be worth "tens of billions of dollars" by the Albanian Agriculture Minister Emin Gjana. In addition, the illegal seizures of government-held lands and illegal construction remain strong phenomena throughout the country, although the government has initiated measures, such as the land reforms in 2006, to tackle this worrying issue.

All in all, Albania's business climate is generally favourable to foreign companies. There are no restrictions on foreign ownership, all sectors are open for foreign direct investment (FDI) and the public procurement process makes little distinction between foreign and domestic firms. Commercial companies are guided by the 1992 Commercial Companies Act, which guarantees foreign companies and investors equal treatment. Albania has also concluded free trade agreements (FTAs) with all neighbouring Balkan countries, thereby easing the flow of products through its borders and ports.

Attracting FDI is a key priority in the country and in 2006 the authorities launched the "Albania for One Euro" scheme, which aims to lure in investors for €1. The government guarantees entry, sites, training and technological assistance for interested companies at that set price. FDI has been rising consistently since 2004, but Albania continues to lag behind in this sphere when compared to its regional competitors.

In June 2007, the Albanian government approved a 10 per cent flat tax rate on corporations, which is the lowest in South East Europe. Other investment incentives are also offered in tourism, especially in construction and redevelopment, where companies may be exempt from profit tax for up to five years, followed by a 50 per cent reduction over the next five years. On a more controversial note, the government also passed a law banning cash transactions of more than €2,228 for businesses, which the government claims is aimed at tackling informality and consolidating the banking system. Many critics have deemed this law an unfair intervention by the state in the business market.

Workforce

The Albanian workforce is still blighted by a brain drain resulting from the socio-economic and political upheavals in the 1990s, which forced thousands of people to flee the country and seek better prospects in the West. A "Brain Gain" programme has been set up by the government to encourage people, particularly those with high skills, to return to the country, and many have returned voluntarily.

Despite clear sectoral transformations, agriculture remains a significant employer of the Albanian workforce, closely followed by manufacturing, construction and trade industries. The labour market is highly competitive, with the lowest wage costs in the region. The national minimum wage is 11,376 Albanian leke (around €93) per month).

Albania's population of just over 3 million includes a working population of slightly less than 2 million. Most Albanians speak more than one language and, in terms of age, Albania has the youngest workforce in Europe. However, education and professional development have in many cases stagnated and this remains a clear threat to the future development of the economy. None of the Albanian universities has been listed on the Academic Ranking of World Universities, although there is a huge presence of private and foreign universities in the country.

Business development and support

Support for entrepreneurs and investors is readily available through various governmental, non-governmental and foreign agencies in the country. The central portal is the Albanian Foreign Investment Promotion Agency, Albinvest, which has been set up by the government specifically to attract foreign investments and diversify current business conditions. Albinvest offers comprehensive information about the legal framework, market system, sectoral opportunities, investment incentives, site locations and other useful details, such as labour availability and taxation in the Albanian business climate. All services are offered for free and the organization deals with all investment types. The National Registration Centre (QKR) provides assistance on procedures for business applications and registration and the Albanian Chamber of Trade and Industry is another useful portal for business support. International consultancies, such as the American Chamber of Commerce in Albania and the Albanian-American Trade & Development Association (AATDA), promote development and trade between the two countries, while the Albanian-British Chamber of Commerce and Industry provides business support and networking opportunities.

Marketing and advertising

The marketing and advertising sector has been developing steadily in Albania, although it is still in its infancy when compared to the rest of Europe. Numerous highly professional domestic and international companies operate in this area, including Ogilvy. Most of them have a diverse and rich client portfolio.

Although international companies make up a clear majority of clients in this area, domestic companies are appreciating the clear advantages offered by the advertising industry to promote their products and are rapidly gaining ground too. The government itself has spent millions in promoting Albanian beaches and holiday resorts on international and national channels. Airline companies, banks, tourist services, beverages and mobile phone operators make up a huge chunk of advertisements, which in many respects reflects the evolving socio-economic structure of the country.

The Albanian TV cable network is highly standardized, being dominated by the provider, DigitAlb, which enjoys a clear monopoly in this area. DigitAlb was one of the first companies to use the latest DVB-H technology for TV transmission in the world.

Despite the evident emergence of an Albanian "upper class", the lamentable fact that most people in Albania are poor is even more evident. Most of them cannot afford the luxury goods they see on their TV screens and therefore remain a price-wary audience.

Part Two

Legal and Regulatory Framework

2.1

Business Structures

Kalo & Associates

Legal framework

The principal legal instrument which governs commercial activity, as well as the establishment and regulation of commercial companies in Albania, is Law No. 7638 on Commercial Companies, which is largely based on French and German company law, and came into force on 1 January 1993. It has recently been superseded by Law No. 9901 on Entrepreneurs and Companies ("the Company Law"), dated 14 April 2008.

The new law has retained provisions that were not repealed and remain in line with the recently approved Law No. 9723 on the National Registration Centre (regarding provisions on the single entrepreneur and on the legal effects of transferring a business name). The new Company Law seeks to provide more detailed regulation on issues pertaining to securities (and, indeed, is intended to be in line with the new draft law on securities), and to focus more on enhancing corporate governance.

Types of structure

The Company Law recognizes and provides for four main forms of business structure capable of carrying out commercial activities in Albania.

General partnership

In a general partnership, all partners have unlimited liability and are equally liable for the obligations of the company. There is no minimum capital required. Each partner can bind the partnership with respect to third parties unless otherwise provided in the statute, and all partners are administrators unless otherwise foreseen in the statute. The company statute (Articles of Association) itself can stipulate that some decisions will be made by a specified majority of partners. Shares of starting capital are not represented by securities and cannot be traded.

Limited partnership

The peculiarity of limited partnership is in the distinction of "general" partners from "limited" partners: limited partners are held liable for the company up to the limit of their contribution of starting capital; general partners have unlimited liability (as is the case in a general partnership). Limited partners may not participate in the management of the partnership and cannot carry out any administration activities, even as a proxy. If this prohibition is violated, the limited partner loses their status and is held collectively responsible as a general partner for the transaction which results from the prohibited activities. In other distinct cases, they may be declared collectively responsible for all the obligations of the company.

Limited liability company

This type of company is the form most commonly used in Albania. A limited liability company is established by one or several partners who are responsible only for losses up to the limit of the value of their contribution to the starting capital, that is to say, the partners have limited liability. It is possible to have a company formed by a "sole partner" and the powers that are usually exercised by all the partners in accordance with the provisions of the Company Law are consolidated and are under the authority of that sole partner. The name of a limited liability company can include the name of one or more of the partners preceded by or immediately followed by the words "limited liability company" or the initials "SHPK".

Limited liability companies are managed by one or more physical persons. Administrators, appointed by the partners, can be chosen from within or outside the group of partners. The duration of their appointment can not be longer than five years and is renewable. The powers of the administrators are determined in accordance with the Company Law, unless otherwise specified in the statute. The administrators have all the necessary powers to operate in the name of the company, with the exception of the powers reserved for partners. The company assumes the obligations resulting from the actions of the administrators, even when these actions are not included within the list of stated objects of the company.

The minimum starting capital for this type of company is 100 Albanian leke (ALL). The capital is divided into equal shares. All of the shares of the starting capital must be subscribed in their entirety by the partners. The statute may stipulate different limitations on the transfer of the shares.

Joint-stock company

A public joint-stock company is a company whose capital is divided into stocks and which is established by shareholders who are held responsible for losses only up to the limit of their contribution to the starting capital. The new Company Law now allows joint-stock companies to consist of a sole shareholder.

This category of company is divided into anonymous companies with or without public offerings. The minimum starting capital for companies without public offerings is ALL 2 million, while, for companies with public offerings, it is ALL 10 million on the date that the statutes are signed. The capital must be subscribed entirely; however only one-quarter of the nominal amount of the shares is required to be paid. The remaining amount must subsequently be paid in accordance with the decision of the board of directors. The Company Law stipulates the conditions for representation and voting by shareholders.

Bodies of joint-stock companies are the general assembly and, depending on the provisions of the statute, either a board of directors as a single administrative body combining the duties of management and supervision (one-tier system), or a supervisory board and managing directors who distribute administrative functions between them (two-tier system). In the two-tier system, the managing directors may be elected and dismissed by the general assembly or by the supervisory board, depending on the provisions of the statute.

One-tier system

The board of directors shall consist of at least three or more members, but not more than 21 (as long as the number is uneven). Directors are natural persons, the majority of whom shall be independent and non-managing (ie. non-executive directors).

The members of the board of directors are elected by the general assembly with the majority present, if no other majority has been provided for by the statute, for a term established by the statute not exceeding three years, with the possibility of re-election.

Two-tier system

In the two-tier system of administration, the managing directors lead the company and decide on the manner of implementation of business policy, while the supervisory board assesses policy implementation and controls compliance with the law and company statutes. The administrators of the company can be elected by the general assembly or by the supervisory board, depending on the statute's provisions.

In the case of matters requiring ordinary majorities, the general assembly may only make valid and binding decisions if attended by shareholders holding more than 30 per cent of the subscribed voting shares. In the case of matters requiring a qualified majority, the general assembly may only make valid and binding decisions if shareholders having more than half of the total number of votes participate in the vote in person, by letter or by electronic means.

Foreign business

The Company Law does not impose any restrictions on foreign companies, whether the foreign company is the sole or one of the founding shareholders of an Albanian company, or whether it acquires shares in an existing company established and organized under Albanian law.

Notwithstanding the above, there are some laws which govern specific areas of activity that restrict the right of either an Albanian or a foreign shareholder to hold a certain percentage of shares in a commercial company. An example is the Law on Television, according to which no one shareholder may hold more than 40 per cent of the shares in a television company.

Representative offices

The legislation allows foreign companies to open representative offices in Albania in order to carry out activities, such as marketing or research, which do not generate any income or profit. Representative office activities are strictly limited to business promotion on behalf of their foreign group, and cannot conduct any commercial operations. However, representative offices can enter into business contracts in the name, and on behalf, of the parent company.

Branches

In order to conduct commercial operations on Albanian territory, branches of foreign legal entities must be registered. A branch is subject to corporate profit tax in the same manner as other Albanian companies, but there is currently no branch remittance tax in Albania.

This approach may be used if foreign investors plan a temporary presence in Albania and decide not to legally separate the new entity from the parent company.

Commercial registration

As part of Albania's reform of its legal system, and efforts to make Albania a more attractive investment destination, the company registration process has been drastically amended. Under the previous regulations, the process was slow, cumbersome and costly.

National Registration Centre

Company registration is now regulated under Law No. 9723 on the National Registration Centre, dated 3 May 2007 ("the NRC Law"), which came into force on 3 September 2007. This law established the National Registration Centre (NRC), which is a central public institution, subordinated to the ministry of economy, trade and energy. The functions of the NRC are as follows:

- to maintain the Commercial Register and perform registrations in the Commercial Register;
- to perform registration of entities for fiscal, social insurance, health care and labour purposes;
- to issue certificates, abstracts of registrations and certified copies of other filed documents;
- to disclose registered data and guarantee free access to the public;
- to accept applications for licences and deliver them to the applicant after approval by the competent bodies; and
- to inform and advise on registration and licensing procedures.

The NRC has established a type of "one-stop-shop" for company registration, whereby one can register a corporate structure for all the relevant registrations (including registration for tax and labour purposes, etc.) at one point of contact.

The NRC exercises its jurisdiction over the entire territory of Albania (as opposed to the previous situation in which companies and the like could only register at the Tirana Court of First Instance). It has established service windows throughout Albania through which it offers its services directly.

The Commercial Register is a unique database of the entities that, according to law, exercise a commercial economic activity. It is kept in electronic form, and registration, treatment and processing of the data submitted to the register is carried out through a computerized system. As there is legislation providing for the legality of electronic signatures, an application for registration may be registered electronically (supporting documents must still be submitted in original hard copy form to the NRC, where they will be scanned). The NRC must issue a registration certificate within the mandatory term of one day from the presentation of the application, provided that the application form is in compliance with the Law. Such certificates, besides the relevant address, also include the denomination, form, date of initial registration and the Subject Unique Identification Number. All data registered can be relied upon by third parties in good faith.

The following entities are obliged to register with the Commercial Register prior to carrying out any commercial economic activity in Albania:

- physical persons performing a commercial economic activity;
- simple partnerships governed by the Civil Code;
- commercial companies;
- branches and representative offices of foreign companies;
- savings and credit companies and unions;

- cooperation companies; and
- any other entity subject to registration in accordance with Albanian law.

Registration of commercial companies

The following data is required for initial company registration of a commercial company in Albania:

(a) name;
(b) form;
(c) date of incorporation;
(d) proof of identification of the founders;
(e) address of legal seat;
(f) object, if determined;
(g) duration, if determined;
(h) proof of identity of the persons responsible for the administration and representation of the company to third parties, their representation competences and the terms of their office; and
(i) specimen signatures of the persons representing the company to third parties.

The following documents should also be submitted:

(a) Act of Incorporation
(b) company bylaws (ie. company statute);
(c) name;
(d) date of incorporation;
(e) proof of identification of the founders;
(f) proof of legal seat (which can be supported by the address stated in the Act of Incorporation or Company Statute);
(g) object, if determined;
(h) duration, if determined;
(i) proof of identity of the persons responsible for the administration and representation of the company in relation to third parties, their representation competences and the terms of their office; and
(j) specimen signatures of the persons representing the company to third parties.

Requirements for a limited liability company

The following additional information should be submitted in order to register a limited liability company:

(a) the value of the initial share capital subscribed;
(b) the number of shares;

(*c*) the nominal value of each share;

(*d*) the participation in the share capital and the value of the contributions of each shareholder; and

(*e*) whether the initial subscribed share capital is paid.

Requirements for a joint-stock company

The following additional information must be provided in order to register a joint-stock company:

(*a*) value of the initial capital subscribed, and the portion paid thereof;

(*b*) number and type of the subscribed shares;

(*c*) nominal value of each share;

(*d*) number of subscribed shares by each shareholder;

(*e*) value and type of contribution of each shareholder, and portion paid by them;

(*f*) special conditions, if any, limiting the transfer of shares;

(*g*) where there are several classes of shares, the information under *(c)* and *(f)* above for each class and the rights attached to the shares of each class;

(*h*) procedures relating to the conversion of types of share, if provided for in the bylaws;

(*i*) the total amount, or at least an estimate, of all the costs payable or chargeable to the company in relation to its formation;

(*j*) special advantages, if any, granted to persons involved in the formation of the company, or in transactions leading to the granting of authorization to commence business;

(*k*) proof of identification of supervisory board members and certified accountants, as well as the term of their office;

(*l*) the number of members of governing bodies of the company; and

(*m*) procedures for appointing members of the governing bodies of the company if they deviate from legal provisions.

The data required in *(e)*, *(f)*, *(g)*, *(h)*, *(i)*, *(j)* and *(m)* above may be provided through reference to the Articles of Incorporation and bylaws, or through reference to the other accompanying documents filed.

In accordance with Article 27 of Law No. 9723, the accompanying documents must be filed as original or authenticated copies, and be comprehensible and legible without any uncertified corrections or deletions. They must also be suitable for electronic duplication. All the documents must be in Albanian, which prevails in the case of discordance, with a certified translation registered together with the original version. It is a requirement that a certified and legalized translation of all official documents from foreign jurisdictions be provided.

Requirements for branches and representative offices of foreign companies

In addition to the mandatory data for registration of commercial companies listed above, in order to register a branch or representative office of a foreign company, the following data is required from the parent company:

(a) value of the foreign company's capital;
(b) name of the branch or representative office, if different from the parent company;
(c) duration of the branch or representative office, if it is determined;
(d) object of activity of the branch or representative office, if it is determined;
(e) registered office of the branch or representative office;
(f) proof of identity of the persons responsible for the administration and representation of the branch or representative office in relation to third parties, their representation competences and terms of office; and
(g) specimen signatures of the persons representing the branch or representative office before third parties.

In addition to the above, the following data is required from branches or representative offices:

(a) Memorandum of Association and Articles of Association of the parent company, if these are drafted in two separate documents, or the equivalent statutory contract in accordance with foreign law, as well as all subsequent amendments;
(b) documentation certifying the registration of the foreign company in the foreign jurisdiction;
(c) documentation certifying the current state of the foreign company, issued within 90 days, with its registration and representation data, including evidence of any liquidation and/or bankruptcy procedures;
(d) an audited balance sheet and audit report of the foreign company for the last financial year, compiled in accordance with the standards required in the foreign country, if the foreign company has performed business for at least one year; and
(e) the decision or other resolution of the competent body of the parent company in accordance with foreign law for the opening of the branch or representative office in Albania.

Joint venture

A joint venture is a legal organization that usually takes the form of a short-term partnership in which the persons jointly undertake a transaction for mutual profit. The venture can also be set up for a continuing business relationship. The parties may agree to enter into a contract that establishes a cooperation or joint venture between them without forming a new legal entity in the typical sense. By doing so, the parties to the joint venture agreement serve their common economic goal by carrying out their activities through the participating entities. Generally, each party contributes assets and shares risks. Like a partnership, joint ventures can involve any type of business transaction and the persons involved can be individuals, groups of individuals, companies or corporations.

Bearing the above in mind, it is necessary to emphasize that the law does not contain any provisions specifically relating to the establishment of joint ventures and so they are not specifically regulated as such. Such joint venture relations can, of course, be factored in when creating a limited liability company or joint-stock company.

Simple partnership

The Albanian Civil Code contains provisions on the formation of "simple partnerships". These kinds of venture are defined as "simple" when they do not reflect the distinguishing characteristics of commercial companies regulated by the Company Law. A partnership is created by a contract whereby two or more people agree to exercise an economic activity with the purposes of dividing the profits gained from it. The contributions of the partners may be in kind, in services, or simply through carrying out the venture's activity.

The general principle of freedom of contract applies to a simple partnership contract; thus parties are free to determine the portion of profits to be distributed. The administration of the partnership belongs to each of the members, but it is possible to appoint one or more individuals to perform these tasks exclusively. Where an administrator is appointed separately from the partnership contract, the obligations of the administrators are governed by the provisions of a separate agreement. The administrators are jointly and severally liable for the commitments of the partnership to the total extent of the partners' private assets when acting in the name and on behalf of the partnership. Unless otherwise provided by contract, the other members undertake the same responsibility. The extent of liability of a partner must be made known to third parties to be effective. There are other provisions within the Civil Code regulating these partnerships.

Registration

To register a simple partnership, an application for initial registration must be filed, together with the required information listed above as well as the relevant contract as provided by the Civil Code and a copy of the identification documents of the members. If the parties have not agreed a written contract, the registration of a simple partnership can be carried out by filing only the completed application form with all the required data and a copy of the identification documents, and by signing the relevant declaration for the acknowledgement, acceptance and application of the legal provisions in force in relation to the organization and functioning of the simple partnership.

2.2

Corporate Governance

Anisa Rrumbullaku, Head of Corporate/Infrastructure, Kalo & Associates

Present situation

The general corporate governance legal framework in Albania is almost complete, despite the lack of existence of a clear set of financial and company corporate governance rules. There are, however, various laws that deal with rights, obligations and mechanisms involving, to a great extent, corporate governance.

On the other hand, the enforcement of corporate governance rules remains rather poor. The major reasons why corporate governance rules remain unsophisticated are the lack of a capital market and listed companies. The recently established Financial Supervisory Authority (as per the Financial Services Law 2006) has regulatory and supervisory power over the securities market, and the authority to implement some corporate governance standards that are laid down in Securities Law 2008. But insofar as no listed companies and no licensed capital market are in existence, these powers remain almost passive, at least for the time being. Nevertheless, Albania, in the course of legal reform and harmonization of its legislation to bring it up to date with that of the European Union (EU), is bracing itself for potential future developments in this area. A recent example is the new National Registration Centre (formed on 3 May 2007). New law expressly introduces the requirement for companies to publish annual accounts. In addition, an Accounting Law (entered into in January 2008) sets forth new financial reporting standards to be applied by legal entities.

Two major projects, namely a new Law on Entrepreneurs and Commercial Companies from the Albanian Parliament in April 2008, and the Law on Securities in February 2008, were aimed at addressing a defined corporate governance framework in Albania in the course of harmonizing internal legislation with the EU's *acquis communautaire*. For the first time, there are specific articles addressing expressly the fiduciary duties and responsibilities of directors, as well as penalties arising out of the breach thereof. It remains to be seen, however, how lawmakers and stakeholders are going enforce the new regulations in these two recent laws in the future.

The remainder of this section will comment upon the existing corporate governance standards in Albania based on:

- the current existing Law on Entrepreneurs and Commercial Companies (2008);
- the Albanian Civil Code (1994, as amended);
- Securities Law (2008);
- Accounting and Financial Standards Law (2004); and
- related secondary legislation.

It is worth noting that the concept of corporate governance was introduced into Albania in the last six or seven years, whereas what may be referred to as corporate governance standards, explained below, mostly reflect those contained in the 2008 Law on Commercial Companies.

Shareholders' rights

Ownership rights

The Law on Entrepreneurs and Commercial Companies requires the maintenance of a share register by a joint-stock company[1] where the information regarding the owners of the shares is registered. The persons registered in the share register are always presumed to be the owners of the company with full rights as against the company and third parties. The obligation to maintain the register falls to the manager of the company and failure to duly maintain the register surprisingly enough calls for the application of certain Criminal Code provisions. Any transfer of shares must be noted in the share register, but it is also mandatory to notify the National Registration Centre as a transfer/acquisition of shares by a person may result in reportable changes to overall shareholdings, ie. more or less than 3 per cent, 5 per cent, 10 per cent, 20 per cent, 25 per cent, 30 per cent, 50 per cent or 75 per cent. Changes to the shareholding structure are also reflected in the Articles of Association of the company.

Decision-making powers

Shareholders have extensive decision-making powers with respect to the election of board members, approval of the company's financial statements and any other such important decision, through an ordinary or extraordinary shareholders' assembly meeting. They have the right to elect or dismiss members of the board of administrators/supervisory board and even

---

[1] Joint-stock companies will be the reference for this article as they are extensively regulated under the Law on Entrepreneurs and Commercial Companies in comparison to other forms of companies.

managing administrators in the two-tier governance system, to appoint auditors, to approve the company's audited annual report, dividends and distribution thereof in proportion to their shareholding.

Albanian joint-stock companies can operate under a one- or two-tier governance system. The first consists of a board of administrators exercising both supervisory and management functions and administrators elected from the board of administrators exercising strictly management functions whereas the second system is comprised of a board of administrators or supervisory board with supervisory functions only and a board of directors with management functions. Members of the board of directors in the two-tier system can be appointed from the general shareholders' meeting or the supervisory board as in the traditional system of the old company law, whereas members of the board of administrators/supervisory board in all cases are appointed by the shareholders' general meeting. The Law on Entrepreneurs and Commercial Companies lays down clearly the powers of both bodies.

Pre-emption rights

Articles 120 and 174 of the Law on Entrepreneurs and Commercial Companies give existing shareholders the pre-emptive right to subscribe for newly issued shares in proportion to their relevant shareholding. This right can be restricted through a decision of an extraordinary shareholders' assembly that requires a super-majority vote of 75 per cent of the outstanding votes of the required quorum.

Right to effective participation and voting

The law provides that the company is obliged to convene a shareholders' meeting at least once a year, and it must be within six months of the end of the fiscal year. Such meetings must be called by the board of directors or the supervisory board, or in absence thereof, upon the request of one or more shareholders whose aggregate shareholding represents at least 5 per cent of the company's issued shares.

The law enables shareholders to participate in the meetings not only in person but also through another shareholder (if the shareholder is an individual) or spouse under the terms of a power of attorney.

As far as quorum is concerned, the extraordinary meeting (where all decisions representing changes to the statutes are taken) requires the presence of shareholders representing more than 50 per cent of the outstanding voting shares, whereas ordinary meetings require representation of more than 30 per cent of voting shares. Approval of decisions requires a super-majority vote of 75 per cent and 50 per cent + 1 in the extraordinary and ordinary meetings, respectively.

Right to be informed and to seek information

Shareholders are entitled to be notified and are able to vote in respect of major corporate changes, such as an amendment to the statutes of the company, issue of additional shares, merger or reorganization of the company, winding up or voluntary liquidation.

The law requires that shareholders be given at least seven (for limited liability companies) or 21 (for joint-stock companies) days' prior notice of the scheduled shareholders' meeting, either through registered mail or e-mail or national newspaper if the company has a large number of shareholders. In addition, together with the notice, shareholders must be informed through the website of the company on the items for discussion or vote, including the agenda, valuation reports, proposed resolutions, report of the auditors or chartered accountants, etc. Shareholders have the right to submit written questions regarding the agenda to the administrators of the company, which have to be addressed not later than eight days before the date of the meeting.

The agenda adopted by the administrators can be amended by one or more shareholders representing at least 5 per cent of the company's issued and outstanding shares upon their request and not later than eight days before the date of the meeting. If the administrators fail to satisfy such request, each shareholder demanding it has the right to claim in court:

1. breach of fiduciary duties from the administrators;
2. purchase of their shares by the company.

Conflicts of interest

In the context of regulating conflicts of interest, Article 13 of the Law on Entrepreneurs and Commercial Companies contains special rules about transactions between the company and persons related to the company. In this context, an administrator or members of the board of administrators/supervisory board cannot enter into agreements or other relationships with the company if such is not authorized by a higher decision making body, ie. the board of administrators. The same is valid for agreements entered into between the company and persons personally or financially related to the administrators or members of the board of administrators/supervisory board. In the same line, a person who is sole administrator and shareholder of a company cannot enter into loan or security agreements with the company.

A shareholder on the other hand is not entitled to vote in the shareholders' meeting if decisions on the judgment of their activity, removal of their obligations, granting of benefits in their favour, etc. are to be adopted.

Change of control

Under the new Securities Law, a company must notify the Financial Supervisory Authority (FSA) of any change of control of more than 5 per cent of the company's share capital when the transfer occurs more than once within a 12-month period. In addition, as many times as a person transfers or acquires shares in a public joint-stock company, the consequence of which results in the transfer/acquisition the total number of shares in the shareholders meeting becoming more or less than 5 per cent, 10 per cent, 25 per cent, 30 per cent, 50 per cent or 75 per cent, notification of the transfer in writing to the FSA becomes mandatory.

Equal treatment of shareholders

The Law on Entrepreneurs and Commercial Companies provides that within a class of shareholders, all have the same voting rights and no distinction is made between different classes of shareholder, ie. minority or foreign shareholders, with respect to voting rights and procedures to be followed at a shareholders' meeting. Priority shares can be issued without voting rights but in this case they cannot represent more than 49 per cent of the company's share capital. Issuance of shares which vests a holder with voting rights in excess of his share in the capital is prohibited.

Prohibition of insider trading and abusive self-dealing

The Law on Securities provides that companies should disclose, without delay, any information which is likely to affect stock exchange prices or disguise the creation of a fraudulent market (Article 95) and further, any person who engages in trading based on information that is undisclosed to the public or abusive, be it the seller, purchaser or any other person related to the company, shall be held criminally liable and forced to indemnify third parties that may have suffered damage as a consequences of such dealings.

Protection of minority shareholders

Minority shareholders enjoy the same privileges and rights as majority shareholders, namely:

- the right of each shareholder to participate in the extraordinary meeting of the shareholders' assembly;
- the right to bring a lawsuit, even individually, against administrators, members of the board of administrators or supervisory board for issues under their responsibility;
- the right to consult certain documents prior to the annual ordinary meeting of shareholders; etc.

Shareholders that own at least 10 per cent of shares are granted specific rights, such as:

(a) the right to convoke the shareholders' meeting if the administrators fail to do so;

(b) the right to include additional items in the notified agenda of the shareholders' meeting at least eight days before the appointed date;

(c) the right to claim in court breach of fiduciary duties or purchase of shares by the company if their rights noted in the foregoing paragraphs are not satisfied;

(d) the right to request from the shareholders' meeting special investigations from an independent field expert regarding the activity of the company when it has doubts that such activity is not properly conducted and, should the shareholders' meeting actively or passively decline such request, request from the court the appointment of such expert for the conducting of investigations at the expense of the company. In addition, the minority shareholders can request the replacement of the independent experts when they have grounds to believe they are is not unbiased;

(e) the right to ask the court to nullify certain decisions of the administrators/ members of the board of administrators /supervisory board decisions where they are deemed to be in material breach of the law and/or the company's Articles of Association;

(f) the right to ask the court to order the replacement of the representative of the company in court when there are grounds to believe that he/she will not act in the best interest of the company.

The role of stakeholders

Stakeholders such as creditors, employees and suppliers enjoy protection through various laws in force, such as the Law on Commercial Companies, the Civil Code and the Bankruptcy Law.

Employees

The Law on Entrepreneurs and Commercial Companies, for example, sets out the right of employees to be formed in Employment Councils in companies having more than 50 employees. The council monitors the enforcement of collective agreements and provisions of the company's Articles of Association. A representative of the company is obliged to continuously inform the council on different company matters, such as company policies especially with respect to pensions, salaries, working conditions, etc. Upon request of the council, the company's representative must make available financial reports of the company; this can be achieved by making the financial reports available on the company website. Unlike under the old company law, the new Law on Entrepreneurs and Commercial Companies does not stipulate that one-third of the positions of the board of administrators/supervisory boards be held by employees of the company. Employee representation at board level is a matter of negotiation between the council and the legal representative of the company.

Creditors

Creditor rights are protected by the Civil Code and specifically by the Bankruptcy Law but sufficiently also by the new Law on Entrepreneurs and Commercial Companies. For example, under this law, a company may only make a distribution to its members if, after payment of the distribution, the company's assets will fully cover its liabilities and the company will have sufficient liquid assets to cover its liabilities as they fall due in the following 12 months. For this purpose, managing directors must issue a "solvency certificate", which explicitly confirms that the proposed distribution meets the above noted criteria, and they are responsible to the company for the accuracy of the solvency certificate. Managing directors who negligently issue an incorrect solvency certificate will be personally liable to the company for the return of the amount of the distribution. In addition, members who receive a distribution from the company where no solvency certificate has been issued, or where the members themselves know that the company can not satisfy the solvency conditions, must return the amount of the distribution.

As with minority shareholders, creditors are entitled to request from the shareholders' meeting or the court special investigations or abrogation of certain management decisions. Creditors also benefit from Article 131 of the law which prohibits a shareholder from requesting repayment of a loan it has granted to the company in terms more favourable than those of the market in times when the company is insolvent and such action would reduce its own capital below the minimum legal capital.

Insolvency law, on the other hand, provides creditors with the right to be involved in the decision-making process in the context of insolvency proceedings through the Creditors' Committee that is created for that purpose, so that they can resolve whether the debtor company should be given an opportunity to survive bankruptcy through reorganization and good administration.

Suppliers

Suppliers and other contractors of the company enjoy protection in the Civil Code either through specific provisions regarding supply contracts or in the general provisions of this Code on rights and obligations.

Disclosure and transparency

Financial and operational results of the company

Under the Law on Entrepreneurs and Commercial Companies, administrators of the company are required to prepare the balance sheet of the company, consolidated balance sheet and progress report to be approved by the board of administrators/supervisory board before being submitted to the annual shareholders' meeting along with a report of the board of administrators for final approval. The board of administrators/supervisory board is obliged to ensure that the company is respecting all accounting laws and standards, including inspecting on a regular basis the accounting books, documents and assets of the company, and ensuring that the auditing of the accounts is performed at least once a year by a chartered independent accountant. The report of the board of administrators noted above must include the board's opinion of the auditor's report.

Disclosure of information regarding board members and key executives

Article 156 of the Law on Entrepreneurs and Commercial Companies requires candidate members of the board of administrators of joint-stock companies to disclose management and board positions in other companies. This is because a person is only permitted to be a member of a board of administrators /supervisory board of a maximum of two companies registered within the Republic of Albania. In addition, a person cannot be member of a board of administrators/supervisory board if he or she is also a chief executive officer (CEO) of a parent company or controlling company or the CEO of another non-related company which in turn has at least one board of administrators/supervisory board member in common. Any position entered into contrary to the above is invalid.

Disclosure of material issues/audit

The Law on Commercial Companies does not require companies to disclose information related to foreseeable material risks, but the Law on Securities, on the other hand, sets out that any company licensed to publicly offer securities in the market is obliged to disclose to third parties any information necessary to assess the financial position of the issuer and avoid the creation of a false securities market, or which can substantially affect the market with respect to the price of securities.

As it stands today, companies have no obligation to produce a corporate governance report together with its annual report or other similar reporting documents.

Financial results of a joint-stock company should be audited annually by an independent auditor and thereafter approved by the general shareholders' meeting.

Dissemination of information

The right to information is guaranteed as a capital right under the new Law on Entrepreneurs and Commercial Companies and for this purpose is laid down as a principle in the body of principles set forth in the first part of this new law. This right guarantees that the persons responsible for the administration of the company must not only keep the shareholders informed on the progress of the company's activity but also provide shareholders upon request with the annual accounts, consolidated accounts, the company's progress report, management and audit report, as well as any other documents with the exception of commercially confidential information. Failure to do so entitles shareholders with the right to request a court to order compliance with these requests.

Under the recent Law on Securities, not only public but also private companies are required to provide information to the Financial Supervisory Authority upon the occurrence of certain events, such as issuance of new shares in specific circumstances.

In addition, the Law on Commercial Companies requires companies to provide to the relevant authority, which at present is the National Registration Centre, any information concerning the following:

- audited financial statements of the company;
- amendments to Articles of Association;
- names of members who are resigning, removed or newly elected;
- names of directors and supervisory board members;
- names of auditors, etc.

The company is not, however, obliged to make the minutes of shareholders' meetings public.

Responsibilities of management

The new Law on Entrepreneurs and Commercial Companies reflects portions of both common and civil law with particular reference to UK, German and Italian law. In contrast to the old company law, the new law embodies a set of principles typically found in common law jurisdictions and doctrines, particularly in respect of the duty of a director of a commercial company. Chapter IV of the law introduces the concept of "fiduciary duty".

Fiduciary duty

Directors are now personally liable in some cases, as set out in Article 16. This personal liability shall apply in situations where they, *inter alia*, treat the assets of the company in a manner as if they were their own and most significantly when they fail to ensure that the company has sufficient capital at a time when they know or ought to have known that the company would not be able to meet its obligations towards third parties.

Non-compete provision

A further change is that there is now a statutory non-compete provision, restricting a director from working in another company of the same profile (during the term of their employment with that company). In accepting a directorship, the director has automatically accepted this non-compete restriction whether or not it is explicitly stated in the assignment letter. This restriction can, however, be waived by shareholders of the company. Breach of this principle, without the proper waiver, triggers the company's right to seek for damages.

Non-disclosure provision

In furtherance of the recognized significant responsibilities of the director of a company, the new law also includes the statutory obligation of non-disclosure, ie. disclosure of business secrets to which they are privy to as a result of their role and duties in the company is strictly forbidden.

Creditor protection

The director is now not only responsible to the company and its members and/or shareholders; the director must now also take on part of the responsibility to protect the creditors of the company. The new law has introduced the requirement for the issue of a solvency certificate, and before distributing profit to the members/shareholders of the company, a director must issue a solvency certificate, and be personally responsible for the accuracy of such. This certificate must certify that the company's assets will fully cover its liabilities, and that the company will have sufficient liquid assets to cover such liabilities as they fall due in the subsequent 12 months. It is clear this provision places additional pressure on the directors, and particularly so in balancing the needs of the sometimes demanding shareholders with the need to adhere to the above rule, although this is somewhat relaxed as some accountability is also placed on the members/ shareholders of the company who accept dividends where no solvency certificate has been issued, or who knew that the company did not satisfy the solvency conditions or, in view of evident circumstances, must have been aware of it.

The above-mentioned provisions clearly indicate that the intention of the new law is to instill significant elements of corporate governance in placing responsibility and accountability in the hands of the director. It also aims to secure the trust of shareholders/members in the company management. This newly introduced principle is reinforced by other articles of the new law specific to joint-stock companies that provide that directors must also perform their duties established by law or statute in good faith in the best interests of the company as a whole, including the environmental sustainability of its operations, while giving adequate consideration to matters to be decided and avoiding actual and potential conflicts between personal interests and those of the company.

Directors' duty of care and skill

Interestingly enough, the law introduces the common law "duty of care and skill" standard where a director must exercise reasonable care and skill in the performance of their functions in the company. Common law doctrine explains that under this principle a director would not be liable for mere errors of judgment and that the duty of care and skill is fulfilled if directors act within their powers with such care as can be reasonably expected of them, taking account their knowledge and experience. The standard is flexible and currently unsupported by any means of interpretation by the Albanian courts to date, and it remains to be seen how, if ever, it will be developed.

2.3

Agency and Distribution

Sophia Darling, Partner, Kalo & Associates

Albania's Civil Code (Law No. 7850, dated 29 July 1994, as amended) contains provisions specifically for the regulation of agency agreements, but not for distributor agreements. The latter appears to be simply governed as a supply or service agreement under the Civil Code (general provisions of contracts). The Civil Code stipulates the principle of freedom of contract, which shall apply to all types of agreements where there are no specific restrictions or limitations provided in the law.

Other legislation which applies to the operation of agency and distribution agreements include:

- the Labour Code (Law No. 7961, dated 12 July 1995, as amended);
- the Law on Competition Protection (No. 9121, dated 28 July 2003); and
- European Union Directive 86/653/EEC on the Coordination of Laws Relating to Self-Employed Commercial Agents.

Commercial agency and agency agreements

As noted above, agency agreements (concerning self-employed agents) are specifically governed by the Civil Code, and where issues are not covered in that section, they shall be governed by the general provisions of contracts and of legal transactions within the Civil Code.

Although Albania is not yet part of the European Union (EU), it is party to a Stabilization Association Agreement (SAA) with the EU that was signed on 12 June 2006. As a result of that agreement, Albania is to harmonize its laws with EU legislation, and so consequently many of the provisions of the EU Directive 86/653/EEC on the Coordination of Laws Relating to Self-Employed Commercial Agents have been incorporated into relevant parts of the Civil Code relating to agency agreements.

Definition

The Civil Code defines the agency agreement as:

> ...one where one party permanently undertakes, in return for remuneration, to promote the creation of and to conclude contracts on behalf of another person within a specified territory.

A person or legal entity that is merely marketing and/or promoting products or services on behalf of another party shall not, according to the above definition, be considered to be an agent, as they are not concluding the contract on behalf of that party. The latter element is crucial to the interpretation of what is an agent, as rules governing agency relations tend to be more onerous.

It is not expressly provided that such agreements, ie. agency agreements between the agent and principal, should be concluded in writing. However, it does seem to be implied as it is specified that each party is entitled to a copy of the agreement signed by the other party.

Exclusivity

According to the Civil Code, the principal may not employ or engage more than two agents at the same time in the same area and in the same line of business; nor can the agent undertake to transact in the same area and in the same line of business on behalf of more than one enterprise in competition with another.

There are very limited sources or tools of legal interpretation within Albanian law; thus it is very difficult, if not impossible at times, to elaborate upon the interpretation or extent to which "same area" or "same line of business" is going to be determined. As with many areas within Albanian law, the interpretation has yet to be tested by the courts. However, the scope of exclusivity within the limits of this provision should be further determined and defined by the agency agreement itself.

Obligation of parties

Although not specifically stated in the specific provisions of the Civil Code relating to agency agreements, the EU Directive on Commercial Agents, the terms of which were reflected in the Civil Code, stipulates that both the agent and principal should act dutifully and in good faith in their relations with each other. The general contract provisions of the Civil Code also provide that parties should act with due diligence in performing the obligations specified in the contract.

Agent obligations

In the performance of his/her duties, the agent is obliged to comply with the instructions given by the principal. He/she is obliged to provide to the principal all information relating to the market conditions in the area subject to the agency agreement, and further provide any other information that is useful in appraising the advantages of individual transactions. The agent shall also conform to the duties that are typically incumbent on commercial agents insofar as they are not excluded by the nature of the agency agreement.

In cases where an agent is not in a position to fulfil the task with which he/she is entrusted, he/she should notify the principal promptly, failing which the agent shall be liable to pay damages. The agent is prohibited by law from receipt of monetary or other considerations belonging to the principal in the absence of an agreement thereof, and if this power has been granted to him/her by the principal, he/she cannot grant discounts or extensions of time for payments due without the specific authorization of the principal.

Customers may address to the agent all declarations concerning the performance of the contract entered into through the agent, and all complaints relating to the non-performance of such contract. The agent can pursue precautionary measures in the interest of the principal and make submissions that are necessary to preserve the rights of the principal.

Principal obligations

The principal has certain obligations towards the agent as provided by the law and in addition to those that maybe provided in the agency agreement. The principal must provide the agent with all necessary information and documents for the goods or services that are the object of the agreement, and all the necessary information for the execution of the agreement. The principal should in particular notify the agent within a reasonable time once he/she has knowledge that the volume of the commercial transactions is much lower than that which the agent could normally have expected. Furthermore, the principal should give the agent notice, within a reasonable time, of the acceptance, rejection or the non-execution of a commercial transaction that the agent has procured for the principal.

Remuneration/commission

The law provides that the agent is entitled to receive commission only for those transactions that are validly completed, and if a transaction is only partially completed then the agent shall be entitled to a commission in proportion to the part of the transaction completed. Unless otherwise agreed, the agent shall also be paid commission for the transactions that have been brought about directly by the principal and which are to be performed in the area exclusively reserved to the agent.

If a completed transaction is dissolved, the agent shall still be entitled to commission, insofar as the completion of the transaction in the first place was as a result of the actions of the agent. The agent shall further be entitled to commission for those transactions that have not been completed as a result of causes imputed to the principal. Should the principal and the third party agree on full or partial non-performance of the transaction, the agent shall have the right to receive a reduced commission in accordance with measures provided in the agency agreement, and if not provided there, in accordance with market customs and practice or failing that the courts shall decide upon the amount.

The principal should provide the agent with an extract of the accounts in relation to his/her commission no later than the last day of the month after the quarter period in which the commission was due. This extract/statement should detail essential elements of the basis upon which the commission was calculated. Within that same term, the liquidated commissions, in respect of the transactions for which there have been payments made by the third parties, must be effectively reimbursed to the agent. The agent has the right to be provided with all information and particularly an extract of the relevant account books for the verification of the amount of liquidated commission.

The agent is not, by law, entitled to be reimbursed for any expenses related to his/her duty as the agent.

Goodwill compensation

Upon the termination of the agency agreement, the agent shall be further entitled to what is termed as goodwill compensation. An agent will be entitled to goodwill compensation from the principal if:

* the principal terminates or refuses to renew the agency agreement; and
* the agent has increased the principal's business with existing customers or identified new customers for the supplier.

The extent of the payments of this type should be considered in light of all the circumstances and, in particular, the commission the agent will have lost from the business transacted with those clients.

Goodwill compensation will not be paid in the following instances:

* the principal terminates the contract due to non-execution attributed to the agent, and, as a result, even a temporary pursuance of the agreement is not possible;
* the agent withdraws from the contract, apart from the cases where the withdrawal is justified in light of the position of the agent in the circumstances, eg. age, temporary disability or any illness for which it

would not be reasonable to expect the continuation of the activity;
- pursuant to the agency agreement, the agent transfers the rights and obligations deriving from that agreement to a third party (though the Civil Code does not permit the assignment/transfer of obligations under a contract to third parties without the consent of the other party or parties to the contract, ie. in this case the consent of the principal).

This goodwill compensation cannot exceed the agent's average annual commission during the last five years of his/her relationship with the principal. If the agreement was for less than five years then the compensation will be calculated as the average of the actual period of agreement. The award of this type of compensation does not preclude the agent from his/her right to indemnity for damages. The agent loses his/her right to goodwill compensation if he/she has failed to request such compensation from the principal within one year from the termination of the agency.

Termination of agreement

An agency agreement may be both for a fixed term, or an indefinite term. In the event that a fixed-term agency agreement is continued and keeps running after its expiry date then it shall be deemed to be an indefinite term agreement. In the case of a fixed-term agreement, parties are free to determine the notice period required for its termination. However, in the case of an indefinite term agreement, the Civil Code specifies minimum notice periods that should be adhered to.

The period of notice cannot be less than:

- one (1) month during the first year of the contract;
- two (2) months during the second year;
- three (3) months during the third year;
- four (4) months during the fourth year;
- five (5) months during the fifth year; and
- six (6) months during the sixth and subsequent years.

Both parties can agree on longer notice periods provided that the principal is not required to observe a shorter period than the agent.

Competition after termination

The Civil Code allows for non-competition clauses to be used in agency agreements for a period after the termination of the agreement, but does set some parameters. A limitation on competition must be in writing, and is usually included in the main agreement. The limitation must relate to the geographical area or the group of customers and the geographical area entrusted to the agent and to the kind of goods, property or services covered by the agency agreement. Furthermore, the duration of the limitation must not be for a period longer than two years after the termination.

Consideration ought to be given to the Competition Law in this respect, as a non-competition clause/agreement may possibly be considered to be un-competitive and thus contrary to the law.

Alternative

There is an alternative to the use of the self-employed (or small entrepreneur) commercial agent, which is employing an agent (in the sense that he/she shall be an employee). This employed agent is one that enters into discussions, or concludes agreements involving any type of activity outside the employer's enterprise, under the direction or on behalf of the employer. The employed agent's employment relations and contract shall be governed by the Labour Code, and any specific Decisions of the Council of Ministers.

Distribution

Definition

There is no specific definition nor are there legal provisions within Albanian law that specifically govern distribution agreements. These types of agreements and relations are usually construed as contracts and shall be governed in accordance with the general contract law provisions in the Civil Code (particularly those relating to supply contracts). A supply contract is defined as one in which one party is bound to carry out an act for the other party in the form of continuous or periodical supply of goods, in return for a price.

Under the principle of general freedom of contract in Albanian law, parties are generally free to negotiate and specify the scope of the terms of the distribution agreement. That agreement shall be binding and enforceable in Albania provided that it does not contravene the mandatory provisions of the laws of Albania, or known principles of law, such as that of good faith.

In Albania, a distributor would not qualify as a "consumer" pursuant to the relevant Consumer Protection Law as it would be purchasing or utilizing goods related to commercial activities or in exercising its profession.

Exclusivity

Any exclusive agreement must comply with the Law on Competition Protection.

The Civil Code provides that if a supply contract contains an exclusivity clause in favour of the supplier, then the distributor cannot receive goods of the same kind from a third person, and nor can he/she, with his/her own means, provide for the production of goods which form the object matter of the contract, unless otherwise agreed upon or provided by law.

If an exclusivity clause is stipulated in favour of the distributor, the supplier cannot directly or indirectly provide any service of the same kind as that contemplated in the contract, within the territory for which the exclusive rights were granted and for the duration of the contract. In order for the exclusivity clause to be binding it must be in writing.

Provided that the agreement is not contrary to the provisions of the Law on Competition Protection, and those of the Civil Code mentioned below, then agreements on exclusivity (to whichever extent) are free to be determined by the parties to the agreement.

Obligations of parties

All parties must carry out their contractual obligations with due diligence and be prompt in performing these obligations in accordance with the contents of the contract. Parties can take advantage of the principle of freedom of contract in determining the rights and obligations.

As part of the general rule of performing obligations, should a party be in default in performing the obligation then that party must compensate the other party for the damage caused, unless it is proven that the non-performance of the obligation was not due to a fault of its own. The concept of fault within the principles of the Civil Code would include acts carried out by wilful misconduct or as a result of gross negligence.

The Civil Code also provides for protection against what may be interpreted as misrepresentation. It provides that during the negotiation or formation of the contract parties must act in good faith with one another. Should either party know, or ought to have known, the existence of a reason for the invalidity of the contract and does not give notice to the other party, then that party is bound to compensate the other for damage suffered by the reliance (without fault) on the validity of the contract.

Termination of agreement

Parties to either an agency or distribution agreement are free to specify the circumstances that justify termination or any related compensation. In regards to a distribution agreement, which is interpreted to be a supply agreement for the purposes of the Albanian Civil Code, where the duration of the supply, or relationship, is not established, each of the parties can withdraw from the contract by providing notice within the time period agreed upon, or in the absence thereof, within a reasonable time and having regard to the nature of the supply.

The Civil Code provides conditions upon which an agreement may be terminated:

- When the execution of obligations is rendered impossible and it is not due to the fault of the performing party, and not outside the time period for its performance the agreement may be terminated. And even then it can only be extinguished if it can be shown that the other party could not have equally performed the obligation if in its place.
- In the case of mutual obligations in which one party fails to perform the obligation, the other party can either seek to demand performance or dissolution of the agreement together with compensation for damages. An agreement may not be dissolved if the non-performance is of slight importance. The law does not specify whether this applies to fixed-term or indefinite term agreements or both. However, the implications of the compensation being for damages suggest that, in the case of a fixed-term agreement, the compensation shall be the remuneration for the period of the term remaining pursuant to the agreement. In the case of an indefinite-term agreement, the compensation for damages shall be decided on a case-by-case basis.

The notice periods required for termination can be indicative of the amount and calculation of the compensation for damages in the case of early termination where the notice periods have not been honoured in indefinite term contracts (for both agency and distribution agreements).

Invalidity

There are also cases where the agreement may be deemed invalid:

- A party to the agreement engaged in a fundamental breach.
- A party entered into the agreement as a result of a fraudulent misrepresentation made by the other party.
- A party entered into the agreement by an obvious mistake.
- Under exceptional circumstances, a fundamental prerequisite (condition precedent) for a party entering into the agreement was compromised.

Interpretation

The Civil Code contains legal provisions for the interpretation of a contract in the event of a dispute. In the event of a dispute, the whole of the contract and individual clauses shall be interpreted so as to have some effect rather than have none. Any ambiguous clauses shall be interpreted according to the general practice in the area where the contract was concluded. On the whole, interpretation shall be geared towards providing for a situation which is most suitable to the nature and object of contract.

Law on Competition Protection

According to the Law on Competition Protection (2003), agreements between companies preventing, restricting or distorting competition are prohibited. These agreements include, for example, direct or indirect fixing of sale and purchase prices and other business conditions, division of markets or sources of supply, or restriction or control of production or distribution channels.

There are exemptions to the above-mentioned prohibition for vertical agreements (ie. agreements between companies up or down the supply chain from one another) that are justified on the grounds of economic efficiency, and have as their object or effect:

- restriction of active sales into the exclusive territory or to an exclusive customer group reserved to the supplier or allocated by the supplier to another buyer, where such restriction does not limit sales by the customers of the buyer;
- restriction of sales to end-users by a buyer operating at the wholesale level of trade;
- restriction of sales to unauthorized distributors by members of a selective distribution system, where the supplying undertaking, directly or indirectly, sells the contracted products to selected distributors on the basis of specific criteria;
- restriction of the buyers' ability to sell components supplied to customers for the purposes of using them to manufacture the same type of products as those produced by the supplier.

Grounds of economic efficiency are determined to be when the agreements:

- reduce production and distribution costs, increase productivity, improve products and production processes, promote research into or dissemination of technical or professional know-how, or exploit resources more rationally, promote development of small and medium-sized enterprises, the results of which cannot be achieved otherwise;
- allow consumers a fair share of the resulting benefit;
- do not substantially restrict competition.

Notification

In order to seek exemption from a prohibition on the agreement, the Competition Authority Commission must be notified about the agreement, or of any changes to an agreement. The notification should include information about, *inter alia*:

- the kind of economic activity;
- the form;
- the content and object of the agreement; and
- the market shares indicating the basis of their calculation and estimation.

Where the Commission finds that there has been an infringement of the "prohibition on agreements" article of the law, it shall request that the infringement be brought to an end. In ensuring that the prohibition has come to an end, the Commission may impose remedies including those of a structural nature.

It is advisable that a local law firm's opinion should be sought as to the effects of such an agreement in relation to the Law on Competition Protection prior to its execution.

2.4

Employment Law

Emel Haxhillari, Associate, Kalo & Associates

Introduction

Albanian legislation provides express guarantees on core labour rights to all citizens, regardless of race, colour, sex, age, religion, political beliefs, nationality or social origin. The right to employment is enshrined in Article 49(1) of the Constitution itself:

> Everyone has the right to earn a means of living by lawful work that he has chosen or accepted himself. Every person is free to choose his profession and place of work as well as his own manner of gaining professional or other qualifications or training.

Given that the Constitution prevails over all Albanian legislation, the labour law, related rights and obligations shall not be effective if they do not comply with the Constitution. As the most important legally binding act, the Constitution defines the principles which are then elaborated in other laws.

Employment in Albania is largely governed and regulated by the 1995 Labour Code (amended twice, under Law No. 8085 of 13 March 1996 and Law No. 9125 of 29 July 2003) which is based on the Albanian Constitution, and in accordance with all international conventions ratified by Albania. The Code provides for the contractual regulation of the relationships between employer and employee by means of individual and collective labour contracts. Foreigners may be employed in the Republic of Albania provided that they have the requisite work permits and residence permits, which are covered by immigration provisions in the Law on Foreigners, the requirements of which fall outside the scope of this discussion.

The Labour Code sets out the framework regulating and applicable to employment matters, the hierarchy of which is as follows:

(*a*) the Constitution of the Republic of Albania;
(*b*) international conventions ratified by the Republic of Albania;
(*c*) the Labour Code and its sub-legal acts;
(*d*) the collective contract of employment;

(e) the individual contract of employment;
(f) internal regulations of the workplace;
(g) local and occupational customs.

Creation of employment relations and contractual obligations

An employer must seek prior permission from the Labour Inspectorate for the commencement of work, prior to:

- creating any new employment position;
- making substantial changes to the manner in which the work is carried out; and
- making use of raw materials, machinery and equipment.

The employer may employ people directly or use the services of state recruitment offices or private employment agencies to recruit employees. However, each and every vacancy must be advertised at the Labour Office and the employer must complete a form detailing the vacant position and the selection criteria.

Forms of employment contract

Employment contracts may be agreed orally or in writing. Certain elements are mandatory and, according to Article 23(3) of the Labour Code, must be included in all written contracts of employment, namely:

- the identity of the parties;
- the workplace;
- a general description of the job;
- the start date of the job;
- the duration of a fixed-term contract;
- the duration of paid vacations;
- the notice period for termination of the contract;
- the main aspects of the wage and the day on which it is paid;
- the normal time of the working week;
- the collective contract that is in force (if any).

When the employment contract is agreed orally, the employer is under a duty to issue a written contract within 30 days of the oral agreement having been reached, bearing its signature and that of the employee and containing all elements listed above. Failure to issue this document in written form will not affect the validity of the contract, but the employer will be penalized with a fine.

In cases where the employee is of restricted legal capacity, an employment contract may only be agreed with the consent of the employee's custodian. In the absence of an employment contract, the employment, for the purposes of the Labour Code, is deemed to have commenced at the moment the employer accepts the employee performing a job for a fixed or indefinite period of time in his organization and implies that wages will be paid in respect of such performance.

An employment contract may last for an indefinite or a fixed period of time, though the employer must provide justification if the term is fixed, eg. the job is only of a temporary nature. Unless otherwise agreed in writing, the first three months of the employment will be deemed to represent a probationary period, regardless of whether the contract is for a fixed or indefinite term. During the probationary period, either party may terminate relations with five days' notice.

Collective contracts

Collective contracts may be agreed between one or more employers, or employment organizations, as one party and one or more trade unions as the other. They may be agreed either at company level or even at sector level, pursuant to the agreement of the contracting parties. The contents of such contracts are usually provisions on employment conditions and relations, content and termination details of individual employment contracts and issues relating to professional training. However, a collective contract cannot contain provisions that are less favourable for employees than those contained in the relevant legislation in force, except where otherwise expressly provided for in the law.

Each employer who issues a collective contract, or is part of an organization that has issued such a contract, shall be bound by its terms and conditions. The contract shall apply to all employees of the employer, regardless of whether they are members of the trade union that negotiated and entered into the collective contract. If an employer chooses to renounce its membership of the trade union that has entered into the contract, it will still be bound until its expiration, but for no longer than three years.

Collective contracts continue to be binding, even in cases where the companies originally entering into such a contract are merged with or acquired by another company. The minister of labour and social affairs may extend the terms and conditions of the collective contract to all employees in an economic sector, when he or she finds that at least one-half of the employees in that sector avail themselves of the more favourable terms of such collective agreements.

There are specific procedures to be followed for the collective bargaining of such contracts, which are not set out here. A collective contract shall only be valid if it is set out in writing and signed by all parties. A collective contract entered into in the form of a written decision issued by a reconciliation office designated by the parties is also valid. The contract must be submitted to the ministry of labour and social affairs within five days of the date that it was entered into, though this is not a condition of the validity of the contract.

The provisions of the collective contract relating to the conditions of the job take precedence over individual employment contracts. It is of particular importance that those provisions of the individual contract that are less favourable to the employee than those in the collective contract are invalid and are replaced by the provisions of the collective contract.

A collective contract entered into for an indefinite period of time may be terminated by either of the parties upon six months' notice. A fixed-term collective contract shall terminate at the end of its duration, as specified in the contract, and any other condition of termination may be agreed in the contract. However, fixed-term contracts exceeding three years may only be terminated upon six months' notice being given by one party to the other at the end of such fixed term.

General overview of obligations

Employee

The Labour Code provides that employees shall personally carry out their duty (ie. they cannot instruct a third person to carry out the job without the consent of the employer) and do so with due diligence, and shall observe the employer's general and specific rules and regulations.They are not obliged to execute and adhere to rules that contravene the conditions of the employment contract or those that endanger his life and health. During the period of employment and the validity of their contract, employees shall not carry out any other job paid by third parties if it would harm or create competition for the employer.

Employer

There are also provisions stipulating mandatory obligations of the employer towards the employee, which are quite common. The employer shall observe and protect the employee's integrity and dignity within the framework of the employment. The employer shall not inspect or check the personal possessions of the employee, except in cases where it is necessary to protect the property of the employer, other employees or third parties from unlawful acts.

More importantly, the employer has certain obligations in respect of health and safety, and must ensure that there are clearly visible signs that indicate where the workplace area may be hazardous to the employee's health and safety. The employer must set out safety rules, and train the employees on all hazards within the workplace that they may be exposed to, and take adequate preventive measures of safety and hygiene. There are also further specific preventive measures that the employer must take against dangers presented by, *inter alia*, substances and agents that are poisonous, machinery, heavy-duty vehicles, air pollution, noise and vibrations.

The Labour Code goes on to impose a duty on the employer to organize, at its own expense, periodic health care visits for employees where the workplace presents certain specific dangers. Special measures for safety and protection of health care are defined in the Decisions of the Council of Ministers.

Working time and leave

In addition to the Constitution and Labour Code, the following legislation governs working time and leave:

- Law on State Labour Inspectorate (No. 7986 of 13 September 1995); and
- Decision of the Council of Ministers on Working Hours and Holidays in Public Institutions (No. 511 of 24 October 2002).

Working hours

Article 83 of the Labour Code provides that reasonable working hours shall not exceed 40 hours per week, and this must be set out in either the collective or the individual employment contract. Provided that the hours worked in a week are within the aforementioned weekly threshold, daily working hours can be more or less than the normal daily eight hours. Within the civil service, as stipulated in the above-mentioned Decision No. 511 of the Council of Ministers, a working week is set at 40 hours and a working day is not more than eight hours. The working day is determined to be eight hours for five days a week but can be adjusted according to specific sectors, for example in the health service working hours are 6.6 hours per day for six days per week.

Overtime and extra working hours are also regulated by the Labour Code (Article 91), which provides that the employer shall compensate the employee for any overtime with an additional 25 per cent of normal payment if time off in lieu is not given, or, if agreed, to compensate with time off in lieu plus an additional 25 per cent of the hours of the normal working day, unless otherwise provided for in the collective contract. Extra work performed on weekends or public holidays will give rise to higher extra payments of an additional 50 per cent of the normal payment, unless otherwise defined by the collective contract.

Night work

The Labour Code also regulates night work, which is defined as work carried out between 10pm and 6am, and which is only permitted for adults over the age of 18 years. The duration of night work and of the work carried out one day before or after must not be longer than eight hours without interruption; it must also be preceded or followed by an immediate break of one day. Working during the evening entitles the employee to extra payment, so for every hour worked between 7pm and 10pm the employee shall receive a payment that is not lower than an additional 20 per cent of normal pay, whereas working between the hours of 10pm and 6am entitles the employee to an extra payment of not less than an additional 50 per cent of the normal salary.

Annual leave and other types of leave

The Labour Code provides for a minimum annual leave period of not less than four calendar weeks in one year (pro rata for those who have worked less than one year). Annual leave is paid. For the purpose of calculating the annual leave period, sick leave shall be considered as working time. The period during which an employee can take annual leave shall be determined by the employer, taking into consideration the employee's preferences, and employees are obliged to give the employer at least 30 days' prior notice of the dates for their annual leave. In addition, where employees receive a salary that includes contribution in kind (eg. accommodation, food and travel expenses), a bonus equal to the contribution in kind, eg. travel expenses to go home, is given. A decision of the Council of Ministers sets out the method of calculation of such additional contributions.

In addition to annual leave, the employee is entitled to other periods of paid leave in specified circumstances, for example:

- for marriage: five days;
- in the event of the death of a spouse, direct predecessors or descendants: 10 days;
- in the event of serious illness of parents and children, as evidenced by a medical report: 10 days.

The law on social security provides for maternity leave, and pursuant to that law a pregnant woman has the right to paid maternity leave of 365 calendar days, including a minimum of 35 days prior to and 42 days after childbirth.

In the case of more than one child, the duration of this period is extended to 390 days. During this period, employees shall receive payment from the Social Security Institute (SII) amounting to:

- 80 per cent of the daily average of their salary over the last calendar year, applicable for the first 150 days of the maternity leave; and
- 50 per cent of the daily average of their salary over the last calendar year, applicable for the remaining days of maternity leave.

Remuneration and contributions

Minimum wage

The minimum salary shall not be lower than the nominal wage fixed by a Decision of the Council of Ministers. Effective from 1 July 2008, the minimum monthly salary for the purpose of calculating social and health contributions is 14,830 Albanian leke (ALL; approximately €122).The employer shall deduct from the employee's salary income tax and social and health insurance contributions, as per the specifications of primary and secondary legislation and of collective or individual contracts. Salaries must be paid in Albanian leke, unless otherwise defined by the agreement between the parties.

Social security insurance contributions

The social security system is governed by the Law on Social Security of 1993, as amended. It covers, amongst other circumstances, old age, disability, survivor benefit, maternity benefit, health care, work-related injuries and unemployment. Social insurance contributions are calculated on the basis of an employee's gross salary. The employer's share is 30.7 per cent in addition to the gross salary, and the employee's share is 11.2 per cent. It is the responsibility of the employer to deduct the employee's share from their salary and to make the payments into the social security system.

These rules must be adhered to and respected by employers, and any failure to so do will result in penalties. There are penalties for failing to register an economic activity (eg. employment of workers), for delayed registration of a new economic activity, for delayed submission of required documents, and also in the event that documents submitted by an employer comprise distorted figures. Penalties are also imposed in cases where an employer has deducted social insurance contributions from its employees' wages, but has not paid them into the social security system or kept records in conformity with the specified procedures.

Each person obliged to pay contributions has the right to appeal against the estimation of additional contribution of interests and penalties. Every employee has the right to appeal in writing to the SII for the calculation of the value of contributions withheld by his employer. Employers and the self-employed may appeal in writing to the tax authorities.

Non-competition and confidentiality

In addition to the provision that employees are not permitted to work for third parties during their period of employment if it would harm the employer or create competition, there are provisions to prevent the employee from working for a competitor after termination of the employment contract.

According to the amendments of the Labour Code under Law No. 9125, 29 July 2003, non-competition clauses taking effect after termination can be enforced subject to the following conditions:

(a) They are provided in writing at the beginning of the employment relationship.
(b) The employee is privy to professional secrets in respect of the employer's business or activity during the course of employment.
(c) The abuse of such privilege shall cause significant damage to the employer.

The non-compete period shall not be longer than one year after the date of termination. Parties are free to determine and set out agreed non-competition clauses in the contract, but they shall only be enforceable insofar as they meet the aforementioned criteria, and the terms of the prohibition must be clearly defined, ie. in relation to place, time and type of activity. An agreement on post-termination non-competition is subject to remuneration for the employee of at least 75 per cent of the salary he would have received if he were still working with the employer. The prohibition will not apply if the employer terminates the contract without reasonable cause or if the employee terminates the contract for a reasonable cause related to the employer.

During the employment relationship and contract, the employer shall not collect information concerning the employee, except in cases where this information is related to the skills of trade of the employee, or if necessary for the contract to be executed. The employee shall not disclose confidential matters, eg. secrets relating to production and activities that he is aware of while working for the employer.

Termination

Procedure for termination

A fixed-term employment contract shall terminate at the end of its term, without the need for any prior notice, although a notice period can be provided for in the contract. An indefinite term employment contract shall terminate when one party decides to so do and the requisite notice period is provided. The Labour Code provides that an employment contract can be terminated with or without cause, and although usually a notice period must be given, there are circumstances where the law justifies immediate termination for reasonable cause.

There are procedures to be followed when the employer decides to terminate the contract of employment, whether it is an immediate termination with cause or with the requisite notice period. If it is following the probationary period, the employer must convene a meeting to discuss the reasons with the employee, giving at least 72 hours' prior written notice. Thereafter the notice of termination of employment may be served upon the employee no earlier than 48 hours after that meeting. If the employer feels that there is reasonable cause to terminate the employment immediately, then the employee may be suspended during this period after the meeting.

Should the employer fail to follow this procedure, it shall be obliged to pay the employee compensation equal to two months' salary, and other possible compensation. The termination of the contract shall, however, remain to be valid.

Notice period

The notice period for termination within the three-month probationary period is at least five days, and this may be reduced or increased by agreement of both parties.

The Labour Code provides for mandatory minimum notice periods to be applied in the case of termination of an indefinite term contract by either the employer or the employee, as follows:

- during the first six months: two weeks;
- between six months and one year: one month
- between one and five years of work: two months; and
- for more than five years of work: three months.

Termination without cause

The termination of an employment contract by the employer prior to its expiry date, without reasonable cause, can result in the employer having to compensate the employee with up to 12 months' salary; the specific obligations of the employer will be decided by the courts. In the case of employment within public administration, if the final decision of the court is to reinstate the employee then the employer is obliged to implement this decision.

A contract of employment shall be deemed to be terminated *without* reasonable cause by the employer in the following cases:

1. The employee had genuine complaints stemming from the employment contract.
2. The employee had satisfied his legal and contractual obligations.
3. The motive for termination was for reasons that related personally to the employee, but did not have any connection to employment relations, namely race, colour, sex, age, civil status, family obligations, pregnancy, religious beliefs, political beliefs, nationality and social status.
4. The motive for termination was due to the employee's exercising of a constitutional right that did not violate any obligations deriving from the employment contract.

5. The motive for termination related to the employee's membership, or non-membership, of a trade union founded in conformity with the law or for reasons of the employee's participation in a union activity that was in conformity with the law.

If an employee is dismissed without any reasonable cause, he has the right to bring a claim against the employer at court within 180 days, beginning with the day on which the notice of termination expired. In the event that an employer is found to have had an unjustifiable motive discovered after the expiration of this deadline, the employee has the right to start legal actions within 30 days, beginning the day on which the particular unjustifiable cause was discovered.

Collective dismissals

Collective dismissal is defined as the termination of labour relations by the employer for reasons unrelated to the employee, where the number of dismissals in a 90-day period is at least:

*   10 for enterprises employing up to 100 employees;
*   15 for enterprises employing 100-200 employees;
*   20 for enterprises employing 200-300 employees; and
*   30 for enterprises employing more than 300 employees.

According to Article 148 of the Labour Code, there are specific procedures that must be followed when an employer plans to execute collective dismissals. The employer shall inform the employees' trade union, recognized as the representative of the employees, in writing. In the absence of a trade union, the employees shall themselves be informed by way of a notice visibly placed in the workplace that shall contain:

*   the reason(s) for dismissal;
*   the number of employees to be dismissed;
*   the number of employees employed; and
*   the period of time during which it is planned to execute the dismissals.

One copy of this notice must also be submitted to the ministry of labour and social affairs.

Within 20 days of the date on which the notice was displayed, the employer shall then proceed with the consultation procedure in order to try and reach an agreement. In the absence of a trade union, all interested employees are entitled to participate in the consultations. If the parties fail to agree, the ministry of labour and social affairs shall assist them in reaching an agreement within 20 days of the date on which the employer informed the ministry in writing, so as to complete the consultation procedure. After the termination of the 20-day deadline, the employer can then inform the employees of their dismissal and begin the termination of employment contracts providing the following notice periods:

- for up to one year of employment: one month;
- for two to five years of work: two months; and
- for more than five years of work: three months.

Non-compliance with this procedure shall result in the employees being compensated with up to six months' salary, in addition to the salary for the notice period or up to the additional compensation granted due to non-compliance with the provision of the specified notice periods.

Transfer of enterprise

Pursuant to Article 137 of the Labour Code, the consent of the employee is required in cases where he is required to work for another employer, where the terms and conditions would be the same as those with the transferring employer. An employee refusing to change employer in this event remains bound by the employment contract until the expiration of the termination notice. According to Article 138(2) of the Labour Code, the previous employer remains jointly responsible with the new employer for obligations deriving from the employment contract until the expiration of the notice period for termination or until such date that is specified in the contract.

The transfer of an enterprise in itself does not generally amount to a valid reason or grounds for the termination of employees' contracts by the existing employer (ie. transferor). The exceptions to this rule are when the dismissals take place due to economic, technical or organizational reasons that impose changes on the employment structure. In such cases, terminations are required and the provisions mentioned above apply (ie. notice periods, individual consultations, etc.). Article 139 of the Labour Law provides for an information and consultation procedure in the event of a transfer of enterprise. The transferor and transferee are obliged to inform the trade union in its role as the employees' representative or, in its absence, the employees, and further explain the reason for the transfer, its legal, economic and social effects on the employees, and the measures to be undertaken in respect thereof. Moreover, they are obliged to engage in consultations regarding the necessary measures to be taken at least 30 days prior to the completion of the transfer.

In the event that an employer terminates the contract without following the above-mentioned procedures of information and consultation, the employee is entitled to compensation equal to six months' salary in addition to the salary he would have received during the requisite notice period.

Trade unions

In Albania, all citizens have the right to join labour organizations for the protection of their employment interests and social security, and all employers and employees have the right to form trade unions (Article 176 of the Labour Code). A trade union must have a minimum of 20 people and is formed as an organization/body with legal status through registration as such with the Court of Tirana. Employee trade unions are organized on a national level (according to the respective industry sector) and also on a company level. Trade unions have the right to negotiate wages, working conditions, etc. and employment contracts that are applicable to both union and non-union workers.

Each legally founded trade union may make a collective bargaining request to its employer or employer organization, in order to commence negotiations in relation to a collective labour contract at either enterprise, group of enterprises or sector level.

Right to strike

The right to strike is provided for by Constitution of the Republic of Albania and by the Labour Code. Employees have the right to strike for the improvement of their working conditions, payment or any other work benefit. Trade unions are entitled to exercise the right to strike for the purpose of resolving their economic and social demands in compliance with the rules defined by the Labour Code. Participation in any strike is voluntary, and no one shall be forced to participate in a strike against his will.

Any action that includes threats or any kind of discrimination of workers due to their participation or non-participation in a strike is prohibited. While a strike is taking place, the parties shall make efforts, through negotiations, to reach a common understanding and sign the relevant agreement confirming the outcome of the negotiations.

A strike shall be deemed lawful if it fulfils the following conditions:

- It is organized by a legally recognized trade union or one that is an affiliate of an organization of employees recognized by law.
- It is for the purpose of agreeing and concluding a collective employment contract, or, if this already exists, the fulfilment of requirements resulting from employment relations not regulated by that contract.
- The trade union on one side and the organization(s) of employers on the other have made efforts to come to an agreement by way of mediation and reconciliation.
- It does not contravene existing Albanian legislation.

There are further limitations to the right to strike; for example, it cannot be exercised in specific situations, such as war time, natural disasters and cases when the right to hold elections is endangered, and if a strike has begun it may be suspended. The right to strike also cannot be exercised in services of vital importance, where the interruption of work endangers the life, personal safety or the health of some or all people. Such vital services include: water supply, electricity supply, fire protection, air traffic control, necessary medical and hospital services and prison services.

A strike shall cease when the parties reach an agreement or the trade union decides to put an end to it.

2.5

Foreign Investment Promotion

Alessandro Boscaino, Associate, Kalo & Associates

Introduction

Upon entry into the World Trade Organization (WTO) in September 2000, Albania applied international trade policy and regulations domestically in order to ensure equal treatment of foreign investors in commercial activity. As a result of this liberal trade regime and a constant harmonization with European Union (EU) custom rules, imports and exports are not subject to any taxes, fees or other barriers, with the exception of any applicable limitations imposed by existing bilateral or multilateral agreements. Albania applies WTO rules on import licensing for specific products affecting life, health and the environment, or with restricted circulation. Although in Albania trading activity generally does not require a licence, in many fields, such as financial services, manufacturing and construction, a special licence from the relevant government ministry or regulatory authority responsible for supervising that business activity is required.

Albania's main markets

The Balkans

Trade liberalization in the region is being promoted by the EU's Stabilization and Association Process (SAP) for Balkan countries. The Albanian government, under the framework of the SAP's Memorandum of Agreement on Trade Facilitation and Liberalization (signed in Brussels by trade ministers of South East European countries in June 2001), vowed to commit itself to implementing liberal trade policies. In accordance with this, Albania has signed Free Trade Agreements (FTAs) with FYR Macedonia, Kosovo and Croatia in recent years. In November 2005, agreements with Bosnia and Herzegovina, Serbia, Montenegro, Romania, Bulgaria and Turkey were finalized, creating the basis for the participation of Albania in the creation of a free trade area in the Balkans region. FTAs with Bulgaria and Romania have been eliminated since they became members of the EU, and an Interim Agreement now applies.

At the summit of prime ministers of South East Europe (SEE) held in Bucharest in April 2006, the Albanian prime minister signed a joint declaration for the Enlargement of the Central European Free Trade Agreement (CEFTA); the agreement was ratified by the Albanian parliament in 2007. Under this agreement, each party is obliged to encourage and create favourable conditions for the export or import of goods and services originating from other parties, and to accord them the same treatment it accords its own products or traders. Albania also signed an asymmetric agreement with Turkey on 21 December 2006, the terms of which provide that Albanian products exported to Turkey are free of custom duties. Simultaneously, tariffs on sensitive industrial products imported from Turkey will continue to be reduced and eventually eliminated after five years. In addition, the two countries will trade agricultural products within the Agreement's specified quota levels with no customs. Standard custom duties will be paid on all products not included above. Albania and Kosovo have entered into a Free Exchange Agreement, providing for complete commercial liberalization between the two countries.

EU market

As a result of the agreement for the creation of a free commercial system in the Balkans, the level of trade between some of the countries in the region has increased considerably; however, the principal commercial partners of Albania remain Italy, Greece, Turkey, China and Germany. In fact, Albania enjoys favourable access to the EU market thanks to the fiscal facilitation policy for export adopted in its favour. In June 2006, the EU and Albania signed the Stabilization and Association Agreement (SAA). The SAA is the central instrument of the SAP, which aims to support SEE countries on their path toward EU membership. The SAA includes provisions covering political dialogue, regional cooperation, trade, movement of goods, services, people and capital, justice and home affairs, and cooperation in a wide range of areas. Furthermore, an interim agreement between the EU and Albania was implemented on 1 December 2006, to further liberalize and develop trade relations between the EU and Albania, creating a customs duty exemption for 83 per cent of industrial products imported to the country. For the remaining excluded products such as hydrocarbons, fertilizers, plastic products, etc., a gradual reduction of tariffs is expected over a period of five years. The liberalization rate on Albanian products which enter the EU market is estimated to be 98 per cent. The interim agreement replaced the Trade, Commercial and Economic Cooperation Agreement between the European Community (EC) and Albania and will be in effect until all EU member countries ratify the SAA with Albania. The EU remains Albania's main trade partner with 85 per cent of exports and 62 per cent of imports. Italy and Greece alone cover 75 per cent of imports and 92 per cent of exports to the EU, or 49 per cent of total imports and 83 per cent of total exports.

Legal framework

Foreign investment is indispensable to sustaining economic growth in Albania, but the infrastructure and implementation of laws designed to encourage and attract investment are often not adequate to support the process of promoting investment. Currently, the Law on Foreign Investment (No. 7764, dated 2 November 1993) exists and has been designed with the aim of creating an investment climate in the country favourable to foreign investors. The law offers substantial guarantees of equal treatment to foreign and domestic, physical and legal entities disposed to invest in Albania. Such provisions state that:

* No sector is closed to foreign investment and no prior government authorization is needed.
* There is no limitation on the percentage share of foreign participation in companies (with the exception of a few areas, eg. investment funds).
* Foreign investment may not be expropriated or nationalized directly or indirectly, except for special cases defined by law to be in the public interest.
* Foreign investors have the right to repatriate all funds and contributions in kind of investments and the object of the repatriation may be the full profit, dividend (after taxation) and funds from the liquidation of a company.

Extremely favourable treatment according to international agreements is also provided. The promotion and protection of reciprocal investments by way of bilateral agreements and double taxation treaties is a common policy adopted by the Albanian government.

Foreign investment in Albania is, therefore, generally permitted and treated according to conditions no less favourable than those which apply to domestic investment in similar circumstances, excluding the ownership of land, which is regulated by a special law. Indeed, the restrictions on the purchase of real estate are notable:

* Agricultural land cannot be purchased by foreigners, but may be rented for up to 99 years.
* Commercial property may be purchased, but only if the proposed investment is worth three times the price of the land.
* There are no restrictions on the purchase of private residential property.

There are a few other exceptions to the liberal investment regime, most of which apply to radio and TV broadcasting, health services and legal services.

In addition, existing legislation governing commercial companies makes no distinctions between foreign and domestic investors. Any investment made through merger and acquisition, takeover and greenfield investment is addressed in the Law on Entrepreneurs and Commercial Companies (No. 9901, dated 14 April 2008), which regulates the activities of companies and establishes the type of legal structure under which companies may be formed.

The National Registration Centre (NRC), opened in September 2007, was established to provide a one-day, one-stop procedure for the entire registration procedure, ie. registration of business entities, obtaining business licences, etc. The government's reforms aimed at improving the business climate also include plans to further develop the one-stop-shop service to include the issuing of licences and permits by the end of 2008.

As further protection for investors, it is important to note that Albania has signed the convention establishing the Multilateral Investment Guarantee Agency (MIGA). MIGA provides investment guarantees against certain non-commercial risks (eg. political risk insurance) to eligible foreign investors for qualified investments in developing member countries.

From the wording of the Law on Foreign Investment and the Law on Entrepreneurs and Commercial Companies, the absence of very detailed incentives for foreign investors other than the equal treatment of foreign and domestic investors is evident. On the other hand, however, Albanian legislation does not burden foreign investors with performance requirements. The only important exception concerning performance requirements is the investment requirement relating to foreigners' purchase of commercial property. Such a purchase can be made only if the investor plans to improve the value of the property by three times the purchase price. Of course it should be noted that for certain commercial activities there may be regulations in place that require certain prior consent/authorizations, eg. activities within the energy sector, mining, insurance, banking and financial services, and licences are required from the respective regulatory bodies.

For the purpose of attracting foreign investment into Albania and in order to support the country's economic development objectives, the Albanian government has created AlbInvest, the state's investment promotion agency. The agency was assigned three strategic goals by the Albanian government:

1. to assist and accelerate the inflow of foreign investment into the Albanian economy;
2. to improve the competitiveness of Albanian exporters; and
3. to provide professional services to assist the growth of Albanian small and medium-sized enterprises (SMEs).

AlbInvest guarantees foreign and domestic investors alike useful assistance to help them meet their investment targets. The following are part of the main services AlbInvest provides to investors:

- updated information on the investment climate, investment incentives and the legal framework relating to the investment process in Albania;
- quantification of the considerable cost benefits that Albania can offer to investing companies;
- identification of suitable greenfield and brownfield site options and/or serviced office space;
- assistance in obtaining permits and licences required by national and local authorities, thus expediting the facilitation of investment projects;
- accurate identification of potential suppliers in Albania.

Other incentives

A new incentive programme for investment in the tourism sector is provided by the Law on Tourism (No. 9734, dated 14 May 2007). The now repealed Law on Priority Tourism Development Zones (No.7665, dated 21 January 1993) had actually introduced more comprehensive incentives. Pursuant to the criteria set out in the stipulations of that law, the investor could have obtained the status of "promoted person" and would have been entitled to profit from a tax exemption for the first five years of activity. Furthermore, for the following five years, the promoted person would have paid only 50 per cent of profit tax. Such persons would also have been excluded from custom taxes on imported goods used for capital investment and would have enjoyed a further reduction of profit tax of up to 40 per cent if the revenues were reinvested in Albania.

The new Law on Tourism repealed the above-mentioned law, eradicating those incentives, and now takes into account the market conditions under which the tourism industry is growing and liberalizes substantially the granting of licences to tourist agencies in a move to increase competition. To further the goal of investment promotion, one of the more positive provisions of this new law is financial assistance through a special development fund for small, private businesses. The fund will be administered by the National Tourism Agency operating under the ministry of tourism. The agency will also coordinate efforts of central and local government, as well as non-governmental organizations and local businesses, to promote tourism.

The new law was introduced to comply with the SAA signed in June 2006 to help Albania prepare for entry into the EU. Tourism is expected to benefit from the interim SAA and in fact, the policy of the EU SAP involves western Balkan countries in a progressive partnership with a view to stabilizing the region and the eventual establishment of a free-trade area.

The latest government initiative, "Albania 1 Euro", is aimed at promoting foreign and domestic investment in strategic sectors of the economy and was launched in September 2006. Its aim and underlying principles are to cut the cost of carrying out and registering business in Albania, as well as to improve fiscal issues, hence attracting foreign investors in the country by enhancing the business climate. Within the framework of this project it is expected that public property (assets, natural resources, economic activities, tariffs for public services) will be provided to investors at a cost of only €1. Institutional and legislative reforms are strongly needed in order for the successful implementation of such an initiative, and the Albanian government is currently working on an action plan for the promotion of investment in the sectors of infrastructure and production, while mainly focusing their efforts on the leasing of public property at very low costs, speeding up the process of immovable property registration, restitution and compensation.

Although Albania has not adopted an authentic private-public participation law, legislation on strategic sectors such as power, water reserves and hydrocarbons provides for the participation of the private sector in such activities. Under the Law on Concession (No. 9663, dated 18 December 2006), the government, in line with strategic objectives, can contribute financial or other guarantees to any project which may be considered participation of the public sector in private investment.

There is also pre-existing legislation relating to the energy sector, which is in keeping with the promotional spirit. In fact, the Law for the Creation of Facilitated Conditions (No. 8987, dated 24 December 2002), concerning the establishment of new plants for the production of power, encourages power production with several fiscal incentives. Investors who establish new production plants with an installed power of over 5 megawatts, using liquid or solid combustibles, and without limitation for other renovator generation sources, as well as the investors who rehabilitate existing plants, will be entitled to profit from a customs duties exemption on imported machinery and equipment used for capital investment. Such investors will also be reimbursed for the customs and excise duties that they have paid during the import of liquid or solid combustibles used for the production of power.

State aid

State aid is considered one of the areas of priority within the framework of the process of integration with Europe. Its obligations are determined in articles 70 and 71 of the SAA, where it is clearly stated that there is a need to prepare the legal framework, harmonized with the *acquis communautaire*, and establish an independent structure that will monitor financial schemes of state aid and individual assistance implemented in Albania. Within this framework, the Department of State Aid was established in the ministry of economy, and the Law on State Aid (No. 9374, dated 21 April 2005) was created with the primary intention of promoting the implementation of important projects and facilitating the development of certain economic activities. The law concerns all sectors of manufacturing and services, and all measures undertaken by central and local governments, as well as other entities acting on behalf of the state that confer benefits to particular enterprises, except those acting in the sectors of agriculture and fisheries.

State aid may take the following forms:

- subsidies or grants;
- exemptions, reductions, deferrals or tax credits and other fiscal contributions;
- the write-off of overdue fees and penalties;
- the write-off of debts or the offsetting of losses;
- loan guarantees or loans at reduced rates;
- a reduction in the price of goods supplied and services provided, including sales/leases of public property below market price or buying products or services at higher than the market price;
- an increase in state-owned equity in enterprises, or an increase of its value.

The law also provides regional aid and aid for enterprises in difficulty.

According to the instruction of the minister of finance (No. 3, dated 30 January 2006), the most significant incentives for investors in Albania are as follows:

- VAT credit at the rate of 100 per cent for importers of machinery and equipment which will serve entirely their taxable economic activity;
- exemption of VAT in favour of fashion producers for services provided to their contractors;
- according to a decision of the Council of Ministers on the Leasing of Assets of State Enterprises Companies and Institutions (No. 315, dated 24 April 2006), rent below market rates for the leasing of state-owned property (buildings, land) and rate reductions for production activity according to investment and employment levels.

Tax exemption

Albania's tax regime is considered by far one of the most important incentives for foreign investment as it is the lowest in Europe; however, the tax system as such does not discriminate against or in favour of foreign investors. Likewise, legislation relating to the public procurement process makes little distinction between foreign and domestic companies, as many activities in Albania require licensing within the territory. The procedures for obtaining a licence are, however, the same for national and foreign companies. The government to date has not screened foreign investments and provided little in the way of tax, financial or other special incentives.

In July 2007, in a bid to promote growth and make the investment climate more business-friendly, the government undertook a major overhaul of the tax system by switching to a 10 per cent flat rate of tax. As of 1 January 2008, corporate tax was reduced to 10 per cent, and VAT and other taxes will gradually be reduced. According to the government's financial plan, these changes should lead to a more streamlined fiscal system. In addition, and for the immediate benefit of the taxpayer, the flat tax rate should help eliminate the potential arbitrage between corporation tax, dividend taxes and income tax, as well as make the economy more competitive, attract direct foreign investment, encourage the legalization of the shadow economy and simplify tax collection.

The tax export regime can be considered a kind of investment incentive for both foreign and national entrepreneurs, and is applicable to all Albanian products destined for export outside the Albanian customs territory. Indeed exports are exempt from VAT (the VAT rate is 0 per cent). Exporters can benefit from a VAT credit for purchases made on behalf of their exports. Overall, if the tax credit for a taxation period is higher than the VAT applicable in that period, taxpayers have the right to use the credit surplus for the following taxable period. Taxable persons have the right to request a reimbursement of the credit surplus when they have a taxable credit amount over three months that is above 400,000 Albanian leke.

As stated above, and since they are essentially exporters, investors are entitled to VAT reimbursement on the purchase of domestic goods or raw materials when it is for production purposes.

As part of its process to establish a more open international market, Albania has signed conventions with many countries for the avoidance of double taxation and the prevention of fiscal evasion with respect to taxes on income and on capital, and these have priority over Albanian domestic law. Tax treaties are in force with the following countries:

Poland	France	Moldova
Hungary	Norway	Federal Republic of Yugoslavia
Czech Republic	Switzerland	Kosovo (UNMIK)
Italy	Romania	Turkey
Sweden	Bulgaria	Russian Federation
Greece	FYR Macedonia	Malaysia
Malta	Croatia	China
Belgium	Serbia	Egypt
The Netherlands	Montenegro	

2.6

Insolvency Law

Ardjana Shehi, Head of Tax and Employment Department, Kalo & Associates

Introduction

The Albanian Bankruptcy Law (No. 8901 of 23 May 2002, amended with Law No. 9919 of 19 May 2008) aims to ensure an adequate, reliable and effective mechanism for the reorganization or liquidation of a company that is facing financial difficulties. The provisions of this law operate in conjunction with other related legal rules, which are widely applied and provided for in the Civil Code, Code of Civil Procedure, the Law on Securing Charges, the Law on Commercial Companies, the Law on the Activity of Insurance, Reinsurance and Their Brokerage/Agency, Tax Procedure Law and in other relevant laws (including laws that ratify international conventions related to bankruptcy). This Bankruptcy Law repealed the previous Law on Bankruptcy Procedures (No. 8017 of 25 October 1995).

The Bankruptcy Law is an evident adaptation of German legislation, which in many respects does not fit with the needs of a developing economy. The Bankruptcy Law directly intervenes not only in the procedural rights of creditors towards an insolvent debtor, but also in the material contractual and property rights of the persons who have legal relations with the insolvent debtor before the bankruptcy procedure starts and/or after it has started.

The Law has been in effect since 1 October 2002. The goal of the law was to establish non-discriminatory and mandatory rules for the repayment of obligations by debtors in a bankruptcy procedure.

Conditions of insolvency

Conditions of bankruptcy include:

- actual insolvency, ie. the status when the debtor is overloaded with debts;
- future insolvency;
- passive status for tax purposes.

According to the Bankruptcy Law, the debtor is insolvent if he is unable to pay the liabilities on the date that they are due. The law expressly provides that the creditor can presume insolvency if the debtor does not execute the payment. The law also provides that the court can accept the initiation of bankruptcy proceedings if the debtor has not paid the liability(ies) within three months after the due date. The law does not stipulate any minimum threshold for the determination of actual insolvency.

As regards future insolvency, the law provides that this is a cause for the debtor (not for the creditor) to initiate the bankruptcy procedure. Future insolvency occurs when there are possibilities that the debtor will not be able to pay the liabilities on the due date.

The Tax Procedure Law No. 9920 of 19 May 2008 contains some provisions related to the opening of the bankruptcy procedure by the tax authorities. The law provides that the tax authorities can submit a request to the court for the opening of the bankruptcy procedure if the company registered with the tax office has the status of the "passive taxpayer" for a period of more than two years (ie. the taxpayer has declared no activity for a period of two years).

Thus, one debtor can *de facto* become bankrupt when at least one of the above conditions is met. The Bankruptcy Law provides that bankruptcy applies to physical persons (small entrepreneurs included), legal entities (companies, non-governmental organizations [NGOs], etc.) and partnerships (simple companies established under a joint-venture contract).

Having taken due consideration of other relevant pieces of existing Albanian legislation, it could be said that other legal entities who are capable of becoming bankrupt are banks and other financial institutions, insurance companies, investment funds, pension funds and state-owned enterprises. However, their bankruptcy is regulated by the special laws relevant to their function and not by the Bankruptcy Law. A bankruptcy procedure may not be initiated for the assets owned by the state or one of its agencies, sectors defined as strategic, or for the units of local government and their agencies.

Bankruptcy Court

Generally, the law does not make any clear differentiation between personal bankruptcy and corporate bankruptcy. However, for the physical person the law provides some different procedures in the opening of a bankruptcy procedure. The law provides for a simplified procedure for small entrepreneurs. The other differentiation is related to efforts to rescue the debtor. The bankruptcy procedure is a court procedure. The commercial sections of district courts (first instance courts in Albania) act as Bankruptcy Courts (BC). The BC performs a traditional role in the bankruptcy procedure and in addition, plays an administration and supervisory role. The BC is in charge of the following main bankruptcy proceedings:

- initiating the bankruptcy procedure;
- supervising the bankruptcy procedure until it ends; and
- supervising the implementation of the reorganization plan.

The law specifies the persons who can make claims in the bankruptcy procedure, namely the debtor, the creditors and the tax office.

The law provides for the preliminary procedure, which begins with the filing of the petition with the court and concludes with the judgment declaring the bankruptcy procedure open. After the judgment is given, the bankruptcy procedure starts to progress. The BC then appoints an administrator (equivalent to a trustee in common law).

It is important to state that under the existing Bankruptcy Law in Albania, any judgment or order of the BC is an Executive Title. The special appeal shall under no circumstances suspend the enforcement of the judgment of the BC.

Participants

In addition to the court, other participants in the bankruptcy procedure are:

- the creditors' meeting;
- the creditors' committee;
- the temporary administrator; and
- the administrator.

The temporary administrator has the authority until the bankruptcy procedure is opened by the court, and the authority is then taken over by the bankruptcy administrator.

The Bankruptcy Court appoints the administrator, who should duly and properly perform, during the whole procedure until it is completed, the duties stated in the law. The law provides specific criteria for the appointment of a bankruptcy administrator. The Bankruptcy Supervision Agency is the institution in charge of training and licensing bankruptcy administrators.

Albanian legislation provides the tax authorities with the right to publish the list of entities subject to bankruptcy procedure; this is already regulated and, in fact, the National Registration Centre is obligated to publicize this list of entities upon receiving the information for the opening of the bankruptcy procedure from the court.

Cross-border bankruptcy

The Law also covers cross-border bankruptcy. The Albanian Bankruptcy Court can initiate bankruptcy proceedings for companies that have a registered permanent establishment in Albania or own an asset located in

Albania. The Albanian Bankruptcy Court may initiate the bankruptcy procedure for the Albanian debtor(s) upon the request of foreign creditor. The bankruptcy procedure is the same as that for any other bankruptcy procedure started by any Albanian debtor(s) or creditor(s). Decisions of the court of other jurisdictions are recognized by Albanian courts, and decisions of Albanian courts are recognized in other jurisdictions in conformity with the legislation of the countries the decision is addressed to, as Albania has not ratified the 1968 Convention on Jurisdiction and the Enforcement of Judgments in Civil and Commercial Matters (Brussels Convention).

It is important to mention that Albanian Bankruptcy Law provides not only for the main procedure, but also for ancillary bankruptcy procedures. The law provides that in addition to the debtor and creditors, the administrator or other appointed representative of the debtor's assets in cross-border bankruptcy proceedings has the right to file a petition to start such ancillary procedures.

Ranking of creditors

The ranking of creditors is regulated by several articles of the law. The law provides that the court procedure shall not begin if there is insufficient money to cover the costs and expenses associated with the procedure. Claims are ranked in the following order:

1. the right of separation from the bankruptcy estate under a title certificate (properties for which a creditor has ownership title are separated from bankruptcy asset);
2. bankruptcy procedure expenses;
3. employees' claim(s) arising out of their employment;
4. secured creditors;
5. unsecured creditors;
6. unsecured creditors of lower ranking; and
7. means of living for the debtor (Article 84) (ie. cost of living, the amount of which should be agreed by the creditors' committee).

In order to meet the court's, creditors' and debtor's expectations, the law classifies and includes as bankruptcy estate the debtor's property, the rights on the date of the initiation of the bankruptcy procedure and the assets that the debtor acquires while the bankruptcy procedure is ongoing.

Alternatives to bankruptcy for the debtor

The Bankruptcy Law provides the debtor some alternatives to bankruptcy which may be agreed upon during insolvency. The alternatives provided by the new law are:

- sale of the debtor;
- corporate rescue; and
- liquidation of the debtor due to bankruptcy.

Albanian Bankruptcy Law recognizes the principle of corporate rescue. The mechanism for implementing corporate rescue is the Reorganization Plan (RP) approved by the creditors' meeting, agreed to by the debtor and approved by a court judgment and filed with the Court Registry. It is the court that supervises the implementation of the RP. The court decides on the termination of the supervision when the creditors' claims are satisfied or their fulfilment is secured, or three years from the conclusion of the bankruptcy procedure and there has been no new request filed with the court to instigate a new bankruptcy procedure.

Bankruptcy consequences

The Bankruptcy Law does not expressly provide for the consequences of bankruptcy. It provides only for the distribution of the bankrupt estate and for the rights of the bankruptcy creditors after the termination of the bankruptcy procedure. In addition, the Bankruptcy Law seems to have acknowledged the principle of "piercing the corporate veil" for the purposes of the bankruptcy procedure, ie. members or shareholders of a company may potentially be held liable for the debtor's liabilities.

2.7

Dispute Resolution

Florian Piperi, Senior Associate, Kalo & Associates

Litigation in Albania is time consuming. It currently takes between two and four years on average to obtain a final and enforceable decision. Optimistically, the government is focusing its attention on the reform of local dispute resolution processes. In addition, as part of the reform of the entire legislative framework in the ambit of the *acquis communautaire*, new enforcement procedures were recently approved and appear to be well drafted and address more precisely the issues that litigants face in practice.

Legal framework

General court proceedings as well as rules of evidence in Albania are governed by the Civil Procedure Code enacted in 1996, amended many times over the years, and also the Criminal Procedure Code enacted in 1995. Other relevant laws include the Law on the Organization of the Judicial System enacted in 1998, and the Law on Mediation enacted in 2003. The rules regulating and governing arbitration are not provided in an individual separate piece of legislation but rather are covered within the Civil Procedure Code. The courts in Albania are an independent branch and provide justice based on the law and the principle of personal discretion of the judges.

Court system in Albania

In Albania there are the following courts:

- the District Courts;
- the Court of Appeals;
- the Supreme Court.

District Courts

The District Courts are otherwise referred to as the Courts of First Instance. Courts of First Instance are organized and function in 29 judicial districts

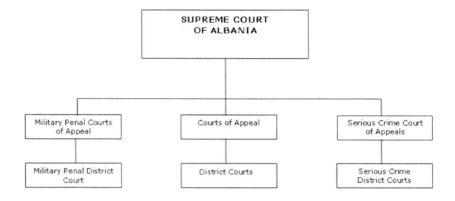

Figure 1. Court structure

throughout the country and one court for serious crimes based in Tirana. In 2007, the ministry of justice, the High Council of Justice and other stakeholders held discussions on reducing the number of district courts in Albania. The territorial jurisdiction of each one is defined by a Decree of the President of the Republic, based on a proposal from the minister of justice after having consulted the opinion of the High Council of Justice. These courts are competent to resolve all civil matters, eg property law related claims, marital litigations, labour law related claims (employment issues, conclusion and application of collective agreements, disputes between employer and trade union, strike issues), tax issues, commercial law related claims, etc.

There are no jury trials under the Albanian judicial system. Customarily, civil cases are heard by one judge only, although the more important cases are heard by a panel of three judges pursuant to exhaustive dispositions.

In addition to general jurisdiction, there are divisions within the District Court that preside over certain matters:

- Commercial Division;
- Administrative Division;
- Family Division;
- Division for Minors/Juveniles.

Commercial Division

The Commercial Division is vested with the competency to preside and decide upon all commercial matters, such as those that:

(a) involve domestic or foreign companies or other legal entities insofar as they relate to their business;

(b) are intellectual property issues arising between legal entities. However, only the Tirana District Court has the competency to preside over and hear disputes in relation to copyright;

(c) relate to company incorporation/registration procedure and all status issues;

(d) are maritime, monopoly and competition issues;

(e) are liquidation, bankruptcy and forced settlement procedures.

On 3 September 2007, a new law setting up the National Registration Centre came into force. The Centre deals exclusively with incorporation of legal entities, and the Commercial Division is no longer involved in the company registration process at all.

Administrative Division

The Administrative Division presides over administrative disputes and is vested with the power to decide upon the lawfulness of final administrative decisions (issued by bodies of the state administration). In deciding these matters, the Administrative Division will adhere to exhaustively specified legal remedies.

Family Division

The Family Division is vested with the competency to resolve all family law related claims such as divorce, child maintenance and alimony.

Division for Minors/Juveniles

This division operates in six district courts only, per a presidential decree that came into force in September 2007.

Courts of Appeal

Courts of Appeal sit in six different regions of the country and review appeals and complaints against the decisions of Courts of First Instance in the respective regions. These courts sit in three judge panels. The courts are allocated in the following regions:

- Court of Appeal of Tirana (covering the judicial districts of Tiranë, Krujë, Kurbin, Mat, Mirditë, Bulqizë, Dibër).
- Court of Appeal of Durres (covering the judicial districts of Durrës, Kavajë, Elbasan, Librazhd, Gramsh).
- Court of Appeal of Vlorë (covering the judicial districts of Vlorë, Fier, Lushnjë, Berat, Skrapar).

- Court of Appeal of Shkodra (covering the judicial districts of Shkodër, Lezhë, Pukë, Tropojë, Kukës)
- Court of Appeal of Gjirokastra (covering the judicial districts of Gjirokastër, Sarandë, Tepelenë, Përmet)
- Court of Appeal of Korçë (covering the judicial districts of Korçë, Pogradec, Kolonjë).

The assignment of cases to judicial panels at all levels of the judicial system is done by lottery according to procedures provided by law. The Court of Appeal will largely look at the merits of case and not only at the lawfulness of the decision of the lower court.

Recently, the Election Code has set up a special panel in the Court of Appeal of Tirana vested with the competency to hear cases brought by political parties or candidates in elections for alleged irregularities.

Supreme Court

The Supreme Court is organized and operates in compliance with the Law on the Organization and Operation of the Supreme Court of the Republic of Albania (No. 8588, dated 15 March 2000). It is the highest court of appeal in Albania and is composed of many judges that are appointed for a nine-year term by the president upon the consent of the parliament.

This Court is organized into civil and criminal panels. The criminal panel tries military and criminal cases and the civil panel hears commercial, administrative, family, labour related cases and the like. For each panel of the Supreme Court, there are five judges sitting.

Decisions of the Supreme Court are issued, with the reasoning behind the decisions, no later than 30 days from the date of the termination of the judicial consideration. Decisions of the Joint Panels, along with their reasoning, are published in the *Periodical Bulletin* of the Supreme Court. Decisions that serve the cohesion of or amend court practice are published immediately in the next issue of the *Official Gazette*.

Constitutional Court

The Constitutional Court was created on the basis of the Constitution, whereas the Law on Organization and Operation of the Constitutional Court (No. 8577, dated 10.2.2000) establishes the manner in which the Constitutional Court is organized and operates.

The Constitutional Court is not considered a chain in the judicial system, but as a special court that acts as a kind of "watch dog" reviewing the compatibility of laws and normative acts of central and local bodies with the Constitution or international agreements, which, after ratification by parliament, prevail over Albanian law. If the District Courts, Courts of

Appeal and Supreme Court, in the course of a hearing, determine that an act is incompatible with the Constitution, they must suspend the hearing and submit the case to the Constitutional Court for review.

The review of such acts may be initiated by the president of Albania, the prime minister, one-fifth of parliament members and the head of the High State Control. Constitutional Court decisions constitute binding precedents for other courts of the judicial system.

According to the Constitution, the Constitutional Court decisions are final, cannot be appealed and must be implemented. All Constitutional Court decisions are published in the *Official Gazette*, together with dissents.

Litigation

Litigation proceedings are initiated by the filing of a complaint/claim to the relevant competent court. The law stipulates that a claim must contain detailed particulars, ie. the facts of the case upon which the claim is based, evidence proving the existing facts and other data (ie. designation of the competent court, names and addresses of the plaintiff and defendant, etc.). In order for it to be accepted, the claim must be in writing and may be submitted either in person by the plaintiff or his representative or by regular post (though in practice the latter option is not used).

After submitting the claim, a preliminary hearing will usually take place at which time a single judge competent in adjudicating first instance proceedings determines whether the complaint meets all the legal criteria prescribed by the law. The same judge shall also decide if the court has jurisdiction over the respective case and can decide to:

(a) dismiss the complaint on grounds of incompetence;
(b) return the claim and other related documents to the plaintiff in the event that the claim does not meet all the prerequisites prescribed by the law; or
(c) deliver the claim to the defendant and schedule a court hearing.

Only the court is authorized to deliver the claim to the defendant, unlike in other legal systems (eg the UK, the United States) where the plaintiff has the right or responsibility to deliver the claim directly to the defendant and a copy to the court at the same time.

The judge in this court of first instance is responsible for the proceedings, and to manage the proceedings in an effective manner without unnecessary delays. The judge is responsible for deciding which evidence will be examined in the court and what facts of the case are to be established. The parties are free to introduce, at any time during the proceedings, any evidence they may find relevant or useful, but the final decision as to whether it shall be accepted is taken by the judge.

Types of evidence accepted by the courts are written documents, facts admitted by the parties in the court hearing, and also witnesses where provided for in the Civil Procedure Code for special cases. An expert witness can also be engaged to provide the court with specific knowledge and information that is in connection with facts that are beyond the knowledge of the judge.

Following the hearing and after having considered and examined all the evidence, the judge shall make a determination and pass a first instance decision.

Appeal

A party not satisfied with the ruling of the court of first instance has the right to appeal to a higher court, ie the Court of Appeal covering that region, and must usually do so within 15 days of the ruling in civil cases.

The court of appeal may either:

(a) uphold the first instance decision;
(b) modify the first instance decision; or
(c) annul the first instance decision and direct that the first instance court re-hear the case (either to establish some new facts of the case or correct some procedural error).

In most cases, the losing party must cover the court and legal costs of the successful party, including the cost of any expert witnesses and the costs of attorney fees. In practice, it takes approximately two to four years on average to complete a litigation proceeding.

Enforcement

After the final court decision has been passed and following the initiation of the enforcement procedures, the losing party has up to 10 days to voluntarily comply with the binding decision. In the event that the losing party fails to do so, the Bailiff's Office may initiate compulsory enforcement procedures. If an enforcement procedure is initiated, the losing party (in an enforcement procedure: the debtor) will be forced to comply with the binding decision and bear the additional costs of the enforcement procedure. The costs are incurred in advance by the creditor, who shall subsequently upon request be reimbursed by the debtor. Enforcement proceedings shall not usually take longer than one year. The forced collection of debt can be made by:

(a) sale of the debtor's real estate;
(b) seizure of the movable property;
(c) removal of the funds from the bank account;

(*d*) seizure and sale of shares that the debtor holds in a company; or
(*e*) any other possible manner.

There are currently new amendments being considered for the enforcement proceedings, as part of the Civil Procedure Code, which are yet to come into force. These amendments are intended to provide a more efficient system for the enforcement of legal rights and remedies and introduce a new system of conservatory measures that help preserve a creditor's position during litigation, and, whilst the claim is pending, also clarify the method of application of enforcement measures to different types of property, eg. shares, movable properties, real estate, etc.

Please see below for comments on the enforcement of foreign court judgments which result from contractual parties agreeing on a foreign jurisdiction and choice of foreign governing law for resolving disputes arising out of their contracts.

Arbitration

Arbitration as an alternative form of dispute resolution is often chosen by international commercial parties in the event of disputes. Due to its efficiency and time and cost-effectiveness, it is also being considered by the Albanian business community as a useful alternative. The Civil Procedure Code provides for arbitration as a dispute resolution mechanism, whereas the actual process of mediation is governed by the Law on Mediation. Contractual parties may elect to have an arbitration clause in their contract, but they still must determine which arbitration procedures they choose to utilize, which venue and what the governing law shall be. Parties may address issues relating to rights and duties that they can freely dispose of, which are usually commercial matters, and thus it is not possible for such arbitration to take place, for instance, in family law matters.

In order to be able to pursue arbitration as an option, it must be stipulated in writing in the agreement, either as an annex or supplement to the agreement or within a clause in the main agreement. The Civil Procedure Code does not limit the choice of foreign arbitration or governing law in a relationship where an international element does not exist, thus foreign arbitration and foreign law may be stipulated in agreements governing commercial operations even where both legal entities are domestic.

The Republic of Albania has ratified and is a signatory to the New York Convention on the Recognition and Enforcement of Foreign Arbitral Awards (1958), therefore foreign arbitration awards may be enforced in Albania, through the court bailiffs, following the Tirana Court of Appeals recognition; it is quite a straightforward procedure.

Recognition of foreign judgments and arbitral awards

In the event that a judgment of a foreign court is obtained, after due process, the same can be affirmed, recognized and enforced by the Albanian courts. The Civil Procedure Code provides, inter alia, that enforcement and recognition of such judgments and arbitral awards shall be subject to the following criteria:

(a) The matter is under jurisdiction of the foreign court having rendered the judgment.
(b) The losing party has been served the lawsuit and the writ of summons to enable him to participate in the hearing to present his case.
(c) No judgment has been rendered by an Albanian court on the same matter and with the same parties.
(d) No Albanian court is trying the same case while the foreign court judgment has yet to become final.
(e) The foreign court judgment has not become final in contravention of the laws of the foreign country.
(f) The foreign court judgment does not run contrary to the fundamental principles of Albanian legislation.

The Civil Procedure Code provides that the Court of Appeal need not consider the merits of the case, but must simply examine whether the judgment or arbitral award is contrary to the aforementioned pre-conditions of recognition.

2.8

Banking Law

Eni Kalo, Associate, Kalo & Associates

Introduction

The history of the banking system in Albania began with the foundation of a central bank (1863–1924), followed by the establishment of the National Bank of Albania (1925–1944), and the State Bank of Albania (1944–1992). The post-war regime nationalized all banking and financial institutions in 1945, and thus the State Bank exercised both the functions of a central bank authority and that of a commercial bank, as it controlled foreign transactions, assisted in the preparation of financial plans for the economy, accepted savings deposits, financed economic activities, and performed other banking functions. The State Bank is now the Bank of Albania. In 1970 an agricultural bank was also created to provide credit facilities for agricultural cooperatives.

The first foreign capital investment into the Albanian banking sector came in the form of the Italian-Albanian Bank, a joint venture bank established by the Bank of Albania and Banca di Roma in 1992. With the failure of state-owned banks to adapt to their new role in a market economy and the collapse of the infamous pyramid schemes, the need to restructure and privatize the state-owned banks became imperative.

In 1997, the state-owned Rural Commercial Bank was closed down due to a failure in the privatization process. Much of its business was absorbed by the Savings Bank of Albania, the largest of the state-owned banks. The National Commercial Bank was successfully privatized in 2000, and sold to a Turkish bank. The Savings Bank was privatized in 2004, and sold to Raiffeisen Bank. During this period, other banks entered the market and a new banking culture was gradually providing much needed oxygen to private enterprise.

In addition to the pioneering Savings Bank (now Raiffeisen Bank), National Commercial Bank and Italian-Albanian Bank (now also controlled by San Paolo Intesa), other commercial banks such as Alpha Bank, American Bank of Albania (also controlled by San Paolo Intesa), National Bank of Greece, Piraeus Bank, Emporiki Bank (now controlled by Crédit Agricole), International Commercial Bank, First Investment Bank, Procredit Bank, Credins Bank, Banka Popullore (now controlled by Société Générale), United

Bank of Albania, Credit Bank, Union Bank, Dardania Bank (now named Italian Development Bank) have since emerged, resulting in a more diversified banking sector that is much more competitive.

The level of lending activity is increasing, particularly in the form of mortgages, and that is due to the extension of various credit lines by international institutions such as the European Bank for Reconstruction and Development and World Bank. Public faith in the banking and financial sector has been restored, as people feel more secure about borrowing and depositing. Another positive aspect is the establishment of micro-finance institutions, which are working within the poorest and most remote areas of the country.

Legal framework

Legislative development of modern banking began in the early 1990s. In April 1992, the Law on the Bank of Albania and the Law on Banks in Albania were enacted, which established the two-tier system with the Bank of Albania performing all the functions of a central bank. Both of these laws have been revised several times since then due to the transition process.

Law on the Bank of Albania

According to the Law on Banks in Albania (No. 9662, dated 18 December 2006; amended by the Law (No. 8384, dated 29 July 1998) on the Addition of a Transitory Provision in the Law on the Bank of Albania (No. 8269, dated 23 December 1997)), commercial banks and non-banking financial institutions provide a wide range of services under the supervision of the Bank of Albania. The Bank of Albania operates as an independent legal entity accountable directly to the Albanian parliament and is responsible for the formulation and implementation of monetary policy in Albania.

Specifically, the Bank of Albania has exclusive power and responsibility to:

- formulate and implement monetary and foreign exchange policies;
- act as the sole issuer of domestic currency in Albania;
- license, supervise and regulate the activities of banks and other financial institutions;
- provide credit for banks;
- oversee the payment system in Albania and facilitate efficient inter-bank payments and settlements;
- hold and manage the official foreign exchange reserves of Albania; and
- distribute securities for the state account and issue securities for its own account.

Its objectives include:

- drafting and revising regulations governing entry to the system and prudent operation of banking activities in the system, monitoring the results and enforcing compliance with those laws and regulations;
- establishing proactive policies and strategies for the supervision of individual banks and the banking system that are based upon an assessment of inherent risks;
- developing supervisory procedures, standards and guidelines that are consistent with international practice;
- implementing those procedures, standards and guidelines consistently;
- assuring the adequacy of staff in terms of number and proficiency to properly supervise the industry; and
- sponsoring and participating in regular communications with the industry and other supervisors on matters of common interest or concern.

Supervisory function

According to the Law on the Bank of Albania and the Law on Banks, one of the Bank of Albania's main functions as a central bank is banking supervision. Supervision of the banking sector is necessary to:

- promote the stability of the banking system and to protect the interests of depositors and the general public;
- ensure a sound banking system whose activities are transparent and governed by the market economy, by:
  - controlling the licensing process, so that only suitable owners and management that are capable of fulfilling the legal, professional and ethical requirements and exercising international best practice have the right to enter the banking market;
  - requiring participants to have adequate capital in line with the risks being undertaken, and to maintain operating risk management and control policies and procedures;
  - in the case of a bank encountering a problem, ensuring that the bank resolves it quickly and efficiently in a manner that protects depositors to the fullest extent possible and minimizes the cost to the government and the public.
- provide an environment of confidence for investors and depositors while enabling growth and profitability for the industry.

It is also the sole authority responsible for issuing and revoking bank licences. The licence is granted for an indefinite period of time and is not transferable.

Law on Banks

The 1992 and 1998 Laws on Banks deal with the second-tier banks in Albania. Albania's signing of the Stabilization and Association Agreement (SAA) with the European Union (EU) on 12 June 2006 led to substantial improvements to Albanian banking legislation, culminating most recently with the 2006 Law on Banks, which came into effect on 1 June 2007.

The new law sets out the criteria and rules for the establishment, licensing, organization, management, conservatorship and liquidation of banks in the exercise of banking and financial activity, as well as supervision of such activity in Albania. The Bank of Albania is charged with the implementation of this law, in accordance with the Law on the Bank of Albania. The new law applies to persons exercising banking and financial activities as defined in the banking law, except for the Bank of Albania and other subjects whose activity is regulated by separate legislation. The Bank of Albania, through its by-laws, has the right to determine whether the subjects listed in Article 126 of the Law on Banks (ie. non-banking financial institutions), exercising financial activities as a result of their nature, volume of activity or the origin of their financial sources, can be excluded from the application of this Law.

A bank is legally established as a joint-stock company and its name must include the word "bank". The minimum amount of initial capital required, paid in cash, in respect of a bank, shall be not less than 1 billion Albanian leke (ALL).

The bank or branch of foreign bank shall be licensed to carry out banking and financial activities as defined in Article 54 of the banking law:

(a) lending of all types including, *inter alia*, consumer credit, mortgage, factoring, and financing of commercial transactions;
(b) leasing;
(c) all payments and money transferring services, including credit, charge and debit cards, traveller's cheques, bankers' drafts;
(d) guarantees and commitments;
(e) trading for own account or for the account of clients, whether on a foreign exchange, in an over-the-counter market or otherwise the following:
  ○ money market instruments (cheques, bills, certificates of deposits, etc.);
  ○ foreign exchange;
  ○ derivative products, including, but not limited to, futures and options;
  ○ exchange rates and interest rate instruments, including products such as swaps and forward agreements;
  ○ transferable securities;
  ○ other negotiable instruments and financial assets including bullion;
  ○ participation in issues of all kinds of securities including underwriting and placement as agent (whether publicly or privately) and provision of services related to such issues;
(f) money broking;

   ○ asset management, such as cash or portfolio management, fund management, custodial, depository and trust services;

   ○ settlement and clearing services for financial assets, including securities, derivative products and other negotiable instruments;

   ○ provision and transfer of financial information, and financial data processing and related software by providers of other financial services;

(g) advisory, intermediation and other auxiliary financial services of all activities listed in (a)–(f) above, including credit reference and analyses, investment and portfolio research and advice, advice on acquisitions and advice on corporate restructuring and strategy.

Banks or branches of foreign banks may not take part directly in industrial or commercial activity, or undertake non-banking services, apart from those banking and financial activities stipulated in the law. Banks or branches of foreign banks will carry out any of the financial activities provided in the law pursuant to the licence granted by the competent regulatory authorities, if any such licence is required by the law in force.

The Law on Banks enables EU member state banks and all foreign banks to provide banking services to Albania, through their branches or subsidiaries, without making any distinction in the licensing terms for their branches and subsidiaries and for Albanian banks. Furthermore, in line with the SAA provisions, the law requires that they be treated as Albanian banks in every aspect, once they are granted the licence to carry out banking business and financial activity.

In order to guarantee and strengthen the protection of depositors and investors and to maintain banking system stability, the banking law provides for clearer rules on the management of risk that banks may be faced with while carrying out their activity. Given the current conditions of rapid credit growth in the banking system, the new law treats fully the other types of risks with which banks may be faced (other than that of credit risk) and the permitted exposures of banks when faced with such risks.

The law requires for the first time, inter alia, the establishment and maintaining of the loans register by the Bank of Albania. The purpose of establishing such a register is to assist banks in making well-informed decisions when extending loans to their clients, as well as to strengthen the Bank of Albania's supervision of the Albanian banking system.

Non-banking financial institutions will be established and organized pursuant to the Law on Entrepreneurs and Companies (No. 9901, dated 14 April 2008). The Bank of Albania, having given due consideration to the specifics of the financial activity exercised by these entities, decides their rules of licensing, supervision and functioning through its by-laws, except where banking law specifically stipulates that it applies to such entities. The Bank of Albania supervises non-banking financial institutions through licensing, regulation, analysis, on-site supervision and a system of reporting by these entities.

Other relevant laws

Civil Code

Albania's Civil Code is based on the Napoleonic Code, the Italian Civil Code and provisions of the Dutch Civil Code. It was enacted on 29 July 1994, and amended on 18 October 1999 and 3 May 2001.

Banking agreements under the Civil Code are deemed contracts whereby the deposit of an amount of money in a bank gives rise to the right of ownership by the depositor over the deposited amount, and the bank is obliged to return it to the client at the end of the term or upon the client's demand. With regard to credit agreements, the Civil Code considers them contracts in which the bank makes available to a customer an amount of money for a fixed or open term.

Law on Deposit Insurance

The Law on Insurance of Deposits (No. 8873, dated 29 March 2002) was enacted in March 2002, and marked a significant step forward for Albania. Pursuant to this law, savings in every bank operating in Albania are secured. Since the adoption of the safety of deposits scheme, the number of bankrupt banks has decreased considerably and, in the case of bankruptcy, the depositors are covered by the Fund for Protection of Deposits.

In October 2002, the Deposit Insurance Agency (DIA) was established with a mandate to protect and compensate deposits in the banking system, but also to contribute to the stability of the Albanian financial system. The insurance scheme insures the deposits of individuals in leke and in foreign currency up to ALL 700,000, with a co-insurance of 15 per cent (up to ALL 350,000 full insurance, and from ALL 350,000 to ALL 700,000 at 85 per cent). Those deposits are insured per depositor per bank.

Deposits are compensated in local currency and must be carried out within three months from the intervention of the Central Bank of Albania in the insured bank. The coverage ratio is that of the financial resources of the DIA to the overall amount of the insured deposits. The financial resources of the DIA recorded a rate of increase of 79 per cent in the period March 2003– March 2004, and the insurance ratio in March 2004 was 1 per cent.

Civil Procedure Code

The Code of Civil Procedure determines the rules for civil and other disputes. The Code establishes special rules that apply to claims brought in the commercial division of the district courts, where all banking disputes shall be tried. In addition, the Code establishes rules of arbitration, should parties agree beforehand to resolve disputes through arbitration.

With respect to banking activity, the Code provides rules for the foreclosures of mortgages in the case of defaulted loans, and provides for summary proceedings and immediate debt recovery through the sale of a debtor's assets through a public or private sale, as the case may be.

Company law

The Law on Entrepreneurs and Companies was enacted in May 2008 and abolished the old 1992 Law on Commercial Companies. The new law provides the legal framework for the formation, functioning and liquidation of companies. The law regulates and governs issues relating to the commercial nature of a company such as the form, purpose, activity, capital, etc. A bank is, by law, to be formed as a joint-stock company and thus subject to this law, but unlike the usual commercial joint-stock companies, it will not have a supervisory body and as such these provisions in the company law do not apply to banks. In addition, it is not sufficient just to be an incorporated company as it can only operate as a bank after having obtained the necessary banking licence, and if it pays the regulatory capital (ALL 1 billion), which is much higher than the share capital required for other joint-stock companies (ALL 2 million). Finally, a company that intends to operate as a bank may not be established by a sole shareholder, but must have at least three shareholders.

Financial leasing law

A law on financial leasing was enacted on 12 May 2005, and governs financial leasing, the rights and obligations of the parties to a financial leasing agreement, and relations deriving from the lease of movable and immovable property. Entities exercising activity as banks or non-banking financial institutions can engage in financial leasing activities only if the relevant licence or authorization therein expressly allows for financial leasing.

Factoring law

Although factoring existed prior to the law, and was permitted subject to a validly issued licence by the Bank of Albania in accordance with the Law on Banks, factoring was recently recognized by a specific law enacted in December 2006. The new law now makes express mention and defines all kinds of features of this specific activity and describes the conduct of factoring, the licensing and the terms of a factoring contract in detail.

Cheques, bills of exchange and promissory notes

Instruments of payments such as cheques, bills of exchange and promissory notes have been regulated by laws heavily based on the French Civil Code.

The Law on Cheques is relatively old, having been enacted in 1963, and has never been amended because of its precision and predictability. Meanwhile, laws on bills of exchange and promissory notes were enacted in February 1996. According to these laws, negotiable instruments must comply with some requirements as to form, which if not respected may render the document and effect to be null and void.

Secured transactions

The Law on the Securing Charges (No. 8537, dated 18 October 1999) entered into force on 1 January 2000, and governs any transaction, whatever its form and however it is denominated, that creates, whether by transfer of ownership, by possession (such as in the case of a pledge) or otherwise, a securing charge over movable property, intangible property or rights of its owner.

Competition law

The Law on Competition Protection was enacted in 2003, and transposes the main EU directives relating to competition issues. It deals with market rules and situations of concentrations that create dominant positions and potential abuse by such dominant positions. It further specifies the role of the Competition Commission and Competition Authority.

Merger control is an issue that may affect banks. The merger control regime also covers the banking sector, and in the case of mergers and acquisitions, Competition Authority notification for issuing a clearance is required (if certain monetary thresholds are exceeded). Non-compliance with the law results in serious penalties that include monetary fines and sometimes forced separation of merger, etc.

Criminal Code

The Criminal Code was enacted on 27 January 1995. According to the section of the code dealing with fraud, stealing property through deception or abuse of trust is punishable with a sentence of up to five years' imprisonment or a fine. Fraudulently obtaining subsidies (or other benefits) from the state through fraudulent information on submitted documents is punishable by a sentence of up to four years' imprisonment or a fine. Fraudulently obtaining credit through fictitious registration of property that does not exist, or that is overvalued, or that belongs to somebody else, and committed with the intent of not paying back the credit, is punishable by a sentence of up to seven years' imprisonment or a fine.

Regulatory framework

Banking licence

Banking licences are granted for an indefinite period of time and are not transferable. The Bank of Albania, through the strict implementation of licensing requirements for establishing new banks, aims to establish a banking system based on sound private banking practices. To that end:

- No entity shall be allowed to undertake banking activity in Albania without a licence granted by the Bank of Albania, the sole authority to issue or revoke licences. The law defines "banking activity" as the receipt of monetary deposits or other repayable funds from the public, and the grant of credits or the placement (ie. investment) for its own account, as well as the issue of payments in the form of electronic money.
- No entity licensed by the Bank of Albania may carry out banking or financial activities outside those stipulated in the licence.
- No entity may use the word "bank" or any other derivative of it in the exercise of commercial or promotional activity without a licence granted by the Bank of Albania except where it is stipulated otherwise in the law or international agreements, or when it transpires from the context that the word "bank" or other derivative words of it do not relate to banking activity.
- No entity whose name is related to the word "bank" and words deriving from it and who has not received initial approval from the Bank of Albania may be registered in the register of commercial companies.

Bank administrators

The Bank of Albania controls the activity of banks, first of all, by screening all bank administrators, in accordance with the relevant regulations and resolutions issued from time to time. Any appointment of an administrator requires the approval of the Bank of Albania.

Money laundering

The Bank of Albania issues instructions to banks to comply with anti-money laundering procedures, including setting up specific units within bank structures to screen evidence and report any suspicious transactions.

Risk control and management

The Bank of Albania issues regulations and instructions from time to time whereby it instructs second-tier banks to be prudent in lending practice to avoid providing big loans (over a certain percentage of the regulatory capital). In addition, the Bank of Albania not only supervises the second-tier banks directly in their everyday business but also instructs them to put in place internal risk control and management structures.

Other industry characteristics

Banks in Albania operate in the market as competitors, but also cooperate with each other to create a modern banking industry and to establish clear practices in banking business. The following characteristics are of great significance.

Inter-banking

The most useful encoded data transmission software for making a payment order within Albania is AIPS (Albanian System of Inter-banking Payments). Reuters Service is the most applicable for inter-bank foreign exchange services with licensed subjects outside Albania.

Self-organization of banks

The Association of Banks and Association of Bank Dealers are two key organizations that play an important role in setting forth the prevailing customary rules and practices in the industry and also in establishing and strengthening inter-banking practice.

Challenges of doing banking business in the era of the internet

E-banking

Internet banking in Albania is not well developed. Moreover, the legal framework is somewhat ambiguous or silent with respect to the provisions of banking services via the internet. The Regulation on Electronic Payments, issued by the Bank of Albania, is limited and states that electronic devices can be an alternative provider of banking products and services to customers. There is no further elaboration or definition of such services.

Compliance with Basel II rules

The Basel II Framework contains measures and minimum standards for capital adequacy that national supervisory authorities are now working to implement through domestic rule-making and adoption procedures. It seeks to improve the existing rules by aligning regulatory capital requirements more closely to the underlying risks that banks face. In addition, the Basel II Framework is intended to promote a more forward-looking approach to capital supervision, one that encourages banks to identify the risks they may face, today and in the future, and to develop or improve their ability to manage those risks. As a result, it is intended to be more flexible and better able to evolve with advances in markets and risk management practices.

2.9

Prevention of Money Laundering

Jona Bica, Head of Banking and Finance Department, Kalo & Associates

Introduction

With the Albanian Institute of Statistics (INSTAT) estimating that 30 per cent of the Albanian economy is informal, the fight against money laundering takes on greater urgency.

Money laundering, the covering up of the source of financial assets, comprises a series of transactions which can be legal or illegal, undertaken in one or more countries. The money laundering process includes:

- the creation of illegal relations with financial institutions through the deposit or transfer of monies;
- the separation of the profit earned from criminal activity from its origin through the use of complex financial transactions.

Economic experts agree that money laundering has a destructive effect on the economy, people's health and the community, as it is the main source for drug and arms trafficking. Money laundering may destroy the integrity of the financial institutions in a country. In addition, money which has been illegally laundered can overflow into the global financial system and diminish the value of currencies, thereby further influencing the national economy.

New legislation

The new Law on Prevention of Money Laundering and Financing of Terrorism (No. 9917), which was approved by the Albanian parliament on 19 May 2008, demonstrates that Albania fulfils (at least theoretically) the 10 strategies recommended by the Federal Bureau of Investigation in the fight against money laundering, which are required to be followed by countries and regions in order to adhere to universal standards already adopted by the international community. Albania has ratified all international conventions related to money laundering prevention and the financing of terrorism. This law replaces the old Law on Money Laundering Prevention (No. 8610, dated 17 May 2000), as amended.

The new law aims to prevent money laundering, products that derive from criminal action and also the financing of terrorism. As mentioned above, the law fulfils international standards and, in addition, creates not only the armature of protection against this phenomenon, but furthermore the capacity for security, discovery and prevention.

The law brings Albanian legislation closer in line with European Union (EU) legislation by fulfilling, at the same time, the requirements of Articles 4, 70 and 82 of the Stabilization and Association Agreement (SAA) and the EU Directive on the Prevention of the Use of the Financial System for the Purposes of Money Laundering and the Financing of Terrorism (No. 2005/60 of October 2005).

The law aims to establish the necessary legal bases for the fight against money laundering and the financing of terrorism, in accordance with the above-mentioned EU Directive on the Prevention of the Use of the Financial System for the Purposes of Money Laundering and the Financing of Terrorism, and also with international standards in this field. The law sets out preventative measures that should be taken by financial and non-financial institutions to prevent the deleterious use of these subjects in money laundering activities or other activities related to the financing of terrorism.

The law:

- identifies entities and doubtful transactions which are subject to reporting;
- identifies the categories of client towards which entities subject to the law must maintain due caution;
- specifies the manner and terms of reporting;
- establishes avenues of cooperation between Albanian and foreign institutions;
- provides for punitive measures in the event of non-reporting or failure to implement measures provided by the law.

The implementation of the law is also intended to achieve partial compliance with the *acquis communautaire*, although, as this was created for EU member states, it is not actually applicable. Full compliance with the *acquis* will be expected in the second phase of implementation of the SAA.

The law introduces considerable innovations in this area. First, the level and mode of supervision of the application of duties to which entities subject to the law must comply (as listed in Article 3 of the law), including on-site inspections conducted either independently or in cooperation with the respective supervisory authority. Second, an annual report by the General

Directorate of Money Laundering Prevention (GDMLP) must be published between January and March of the year following the reporting year and must be publicly available. This report must include detailed information regarding the source of all reported statistics and data and also the results of cases investigated by the Public Prosecutor's office. A considerable number of positive financial effects are expected to result from the implementation of this law.

General Directorate of Money Laundering Prevention

The GDMLP, formerly within the ministry of finance but now an independent agency, is the competent authority for the prevention of money laundering. It is Albania's specialist financial unit and is tasked with supervising and analysing implementation of the law by various agencies and entities. The GDMLP supervises the reporting entities which are subject to the law.

In comparison with the old law:

- The number of reporting entities subject to the law has increased.
- The monetary threshold to be declared by reporting entities subject to the law has decreased.
- The number of measures to be taken by reporting entities subject to the law has increased.
- The provision and regulation of measures for the prevention of the financing of terrorism have been introduced for the first time.

Requirements of the law

According to Article 4, those entities which are subject to the law have an obligation to identify clients and verify their identity through identification documents in the following cases:

1. before they establish business relations;
2. when a client in cases other than those referred to in (1) above performs or wishes to perform:
   (a) a money transfer within or outside the country; or
   (b) a transaction in an amount equal to:
      ○ no less than 200,000 Albanian leke (ALL) or its corresponding value in a foreign currency for the sale/purchase of gambling chips, or their corresponding electronic value in the case of gambling, casinos and hippodromes (race tracks) of any kind; or
      ○ no less than ALL 1.5 million or its corresponding value in a foreign currency performed in a sole transaction or in different but related transactions. If the amount of the transactions is not

known during the action, the identification must be made immediately after the amount is known and the above-mentioned threshold is met;

3. when there is doubt surrounding the veracity of identification data provided in the past;
4. in all cases where there exists evidence or sufficient suspicion of money-laundering activity and/or the financing of terrorism.

Reporting to the GDMLP

Those entities subject to the law are also obligated to identify the proprietor beneficiary of these amounts.

Those entities subject to the law are required to report directly to the GDMLP when they suspect that a property is a product of criminal activity or is going to be used to finance terrorism. When an entity subject to the law is asked by a client to perform a transaction for which the entity has sufficient suspicion, it must report it to the GDMLP and ask for instructions as to whether it should conclude the transaction. The GDMLP must reply within 48 hours.

Those entities subject to the law are required to report to the GDMLP, in accordance with the prescribed terms in the by-laws issued for the implementation of this law, as follows:

- all transactions in cash of a value equal to or greater than ALL 1.5 million or its corresponding value in a foreign currency; and
- all non-cash transactions, with a value equal to or greater than ALL 6 million or its corresponding value in a foreign currency, performed in a single or in different but related transactions.

2.10

Competition Law

Jona Bica, Head of Banking and Finance Department, Kalo & Associate

Introduction

The Albanian economy is experiencing dynamic changes, including in particular the development of a modern market place. Competition is an essential component of these changes, as it brings the necessity for the establishment of a modern legal and institutional framework to be developed in harmony with European Union (EU) legislation. The basis for the implementation of a modern competition policy in Albania has now been established. Albanian competition legislation was adapted not only to incorporate EU competition-related legislation but also to meet the contemporary requirements of the developing Albanian market.

The current competition framework is governed primarily by the Law on Protection of Competition (No. 9121, 28 July 2003), and also supplementary relevant regulations and instructions.

The Competition Law provided for the establishment of the Competition Authority, which is the authorized body designated to implement the provisions of the Law. It is a public entity independent in performing its tasks, and comprised of two bodies, the Commission and the Secretariat. The Commission is the decision-making body of the Authority (elected by the parliament), and is comprised of five members, whereas the Secretariat is the administrative and investigative body (ie. having market monitoring and investigative powers). The duties and responsibilities of each body are regulated by competition law.

The Competition Law is aimed at the protection of a fair and effective market, defining the rules of conduct by undertakings, as well as the institutions responsible for the protection of competition.

This law applies regardless of whether or not the undertakings are registered, based, or have subsidiaries within the territory of Albania. The key factor is whether such undertakings perform activities within the territory of Albania and, as a consequence of such activity, the domestic market is affected. The exercise of economic activities includes any type of manufacturing, commercial, financial or professional activity associated with the purchase or sale of goods, as well as the offering of a service within Albania.

The law applies to agreements and concentrations between entities engaged in commercial activity.

Agreements

Competition law applies to any type of agreement, either formal or informal, tacit or explicit, horizontal (ie. agreements between entities operating on the same level of production) or vertical (ie. agreements between entities operating on different levels of production) which may prevent, restrict or distort competition in the market.

Strict prohibitions

The law identifies strictly prohibited agreements, namely those that:

- directly or indirectly fix the purchase or sale price, or any other trading conditions;
- limit or control production, markets, technical development or investment;
- share market or sources of supply;
- apply dissimilar conditions to equivalent transactions with other trading parties, thereby placing them at a competitive disadvantage;
- make the conclusion of contracts subject to acceptance by the other parties of supplementary obligations, which, by their nature or according to commercial usage, have no connection with the subject of such contracts.

Exemptions from prohibitions

The law also specifies certain other agreements that are prohibited, but these can qualify for exemption from such prohibition, provided that they fulfil certain criteria as described below. Such agreements are as follows:

- horizontal agreements, which have, in particular, as their object or effect the specialization or rationalization of economic activity, the research and development of products and processes, the joint purchasing or sale of products from and to a single source, provided that they are justified on the grounds of economic efficiency;
- vertical agreements, which are justified on the grounds of economic efficiency, and have, in particular, as their object or effect:
  - the restriction of active sales into an exclusive territory or to an exclusive customer group reserved to the supplier or allocated by the supplier to another buyer, where such a restriction does not limit sales by the customers of the buyer;

- ○ the restriction of sales to end-users by a buyer operating on the wholesale level of trade;
- ○ the restriction of sales to unauthorized distributors by the members of a selective distribution system, where the supply undertaking, directly or indirectly, sells the contracted products to selected distributors on the basis of specific criteria;
- ○ the restriction of the buyers' ability to sell components supplied to customers for the purposes of using them to manufacture the same type of products as those produced by the supplier.

Economic efficiency

Economic efficiency is deemed to be justified when the agreements:

- reduce production and distribution costs, increase productivity, improve products or production processes, promote research into or dissemination of technical or professional know-how, or exploit resources more rationally, promote the development of small and medium enterprises or promote the development of results which cannot be achieved otherwise;
- allow consumers a fair share of the resulting benefit;
- do not substantially restrict competition.

In order to seek exemption from prohibition, the Competition Authority must be notified about agreements or of any changes to existing agreements. The notification should include information on inter alia the type of economic activity, form, content and object of agreement and market shares, indicating the basis of their calculation and estimation. Exemptions are limited in time and may be granted to undertakings subject to certain conditions and obligations. While the law provides for specific treatment of agreements on intellectual and industrial property rights, for which the exemption is granted automatically, if the Competition Authority does not reply within three months of the notification, all other agreements falling within those that are eligible for exemption must by law be explicitly exempted.

Notification forms shall include the following particulars:

(a) name or other designation and place of business or registered seat of the participating undertakings;
(b) type of economic activity;
(c) form, content and object of the agreements;
(d) market shares of the undertakings indicating the basis of their calculation and estimation;
(e) the person authorized to represent the undertaking during the procedures.

Note that the new law does not provide an exhaustive list of agreements that are not restrictive of competition *per se*. It remains at the discretion of the Competition Authority to deal with agreements that do not fall under either the aforementioned strictly prohibited agreements or those that are eligible for exemption.

See below for language requirements of the notification form.

Abuse of a dominant market position

The dominant position of one or more undertakings shall be determined in particular by establishing:

- the relevant market share of the undertaking and that of other competitors;
- barriers to entry to the relevant market;
- potential competition;
- the economic and financial power of the undertaking;
- the economic dependence of suppliers and purchasers;
- the countervailing power of buyers/customers;
- the development of the undertaking's distribution network, and access to the sources of supply of products;
- the undertaking's connections with other undertakings;
- other characteristics of the relevant market, such as the homogeneity of the products, the transparency of the market, the undertaking's cost and size symmetries, the stability of demand or free production capacities.

Any abuse by one or more undertakings of a dominant position in the market is prohibited. Abuses of a dominant position consist of:

- directly or indirectly imposing unfair purchase or selling prices or other unfair trading conditions;
- limiting production, markets or technical development;
- applying dissimilar conditions to equivalent transactions with other trading parties, thereby placing them at a competitive disadvantage;
- making the conclusion of contracts subject to acceptance by other parties of supplementary obligations;
- undercutting prices or other conditions that have as their object or effect the prevention of entry to or the expulsion from the market for specific competitor(s) or one of their products;
- refusing to deal or refusing to license;
- refusing to allow another undertaking access to its own networks or other infrastructure facilities of undertakings with a dominant position, against adequate remuneration, provided that without such concurrent use the other undertaking is unable to operate as a competitor of the undertaking with a dominant position.

Practices of one or more undertakings with a dominant position in the market shall not be considered abusive if such undertakings prove that these practices are performed for objective reasons, eg technical or legal/ commercial reasons.

Concentrations

Definition

The definition provided in the Competition Law for a concentration of undertakings is:

(a) the merger of two or more undertakings (which are private or public legal entities performing an economic activity, which includes "sales") or parts of undertakings that have been, up to the point of merger, independent of each other; or
(b) any transaction where one or more undertakings acquire, directly or indirectly, a controlling interest in all or parts of one or more of other undertakings; or
(c) joint ventures exercising all functions of an autonomous economic entity.

Transactions that result in a concentration of undertakings must be reported to the competent authority, in this case the Competition Authority, only if certain thresholds of turnover of the respective companies are exceeded.

There are no differences in the application of competition law in Albania, ie. whether the transaction is by way of a merger, acquisition or public takeover. According to this law, any joint venture that performs the function of an independent economic unit is also subject to these provisions.

Notification thresholds

The notification thresholds for the intended transaction (ie. which will result in a concentration of undertakings) are as follows (the figures are taken from the business year preceding the intended transaction):

1. The combined worldwide turnover of all participating undertakings is more than 70 billion Albanian leke (ALL), or the domestic combined turnover of all participating undertakings in Albania is more than ALL 800 million.
2. The turnover of at least one participating undertaking in Albania is more than ALL 500 million.

As the notification to the Competition Authority is made prior to the completion of the intended transaction, the exchange rate that would be used to convert the turnover from the currency of the original currency into ALL is the exchange rate on the date that the notification is submitted to the Competition Authority.

Aggregate turnover will comprise the amount derived by the undertaking in the preceding business year from the sale of products falling within the undertaking's ordinary activities, after deduction of taxes directly related to the turnover.

Where the above notification thresholds are met, the filing of the notification in Albania is mandatory and there are no exceptions to this rule.

Foreign to foreign mergers are subject to notification when at least one of the parties has a duly registered branch or a representative office in Albania. Filing a notification is required even when the target does not have a registered entity in Albania but does export to Albania.

Pre-notification discussions with the Competition Authority

The Law does not provide for pre-notification discussions with the Competition Authority before a filing is made, though in practice this is possible with representatives from the Competition Authority. The information given to the Authority could be of a general nature and, certainly, at any time the right not to disclose confidential information (even the company name(s)) remains with the representatives of the companies making the notification. Such pre-notification enquiries, however general in nature, can prove to be very useful when contemplating mergers, joint ventures or engaging in agreements that may be considered to be anti-competitive.

Pre-notification phase

In practice, the usual preparation time for a merger notification in Albania takes some one to two weeks (ie. to retrieve the application form from the Authority, to translate and notarize the documents that will be attached to the notification and to submit the notification to the specific department of the Authority, and other steps as may be deemed appropriate). This period begins the moment that the local law firm receives all relevant documents, including those that require apostille stamps, but it will depend on the quantity of papers required to be translated.

Notifying party/parties

The obligation for notification falls on all the companies that are party to a merger agreement. The regulations of the Competition Authority provide for joint notification(s). In this case, the companies should provide written authorization that only one single person shall act as the authorized representative and shall have the powers to follow the procedure. The parties that make the notification, or their representatives, should have an address in Albania that will be used for correspondence purposes. Joint notifications should be submitted using one single form. In the case of acquisition of the controlling interest in a company, notification shall be filled in and submitted by the purchaser.

Timetable for filing and the issue of the decision

The filing of the notification must be made within one week from the conclusion of an agreement to merge, the acquisition of a controlling interest or the announcement of a public bid. The law does not provide for any possible extension of this one-week term.

The Competition Authority must render its initial decision within two months of receiving a notification, if it finds that the merger does not have any sign of a dominant position in the market. This period can be extended for an additional two weeks in cases of conditional clearance (ie. a total of two months and two weeks).

On receipt of notification, the Competition Authority gives written notice to the companies advising whether the notification is properly completed or not. In cases where the notification is deemed incomplete, the Competition Authority grants a period of time for the completion of notification.

If the Competition Authority fails to take any decision within two months of the notification, and the parties are not notified, then the proposed concentration shall, by this silence, be deemed to be effective and operational.

If the Authority decides that the merger may create dominance in the market, it shall proceed with an in-depth procedure and must issue a decision within three months of the decision to start such procedure. This three-month period starts on the date the decision for the in-depth procedure is given, and can be extended for an additional one month in cases of conditional clearance.

Obligations to suspend

Implementation of the transaction must be suspended until clearance by the Competition Authority and until conditions attached to an authorization or request(s) from the Authority have been fulfilled.

The law does not specifically provide for conditions under which exemptions from such suspensions are granted. However, an exemption from the obligation to suspend can be obtained if the parties are required to close the transaction globally before they are able to obtain approval in Albania. Following the logic of the provisions of the law and regulations on competition and, in particular, the provisions dealing with the relations that the Competition Authority has with the relevant authority in the European

Commission and similar authorities in other countries, the above justification is quite a reasonable and lawful one for obtaining such an exemption.

Language

The notification form must be submitted in Albanian. Each of the documents to be submitted to the Competition Authority must be in the official language of the country in which the company is based. In the case that its official language is neither Albanian nor English, an official translation in Albanian, certified by a notary public, must be attached to the notification.

In the case that the legal person that makes the notification does not have any permanent establishment in Albania, the Competition Authority may authorize the notifying parties to make the notification in English.

The documents attached to the notification should contain at least one original and two copies certified by the notary public. The original official documents should be notarized with anapostille stamp, ie. if they are provided by a company duly registered in a country that is a signatory to the Hague Convention. If the country is not a signatory to the Hague Convention, the official documents should be legalized by the competent body of that country.

Documents that are considered confidential should be marked "Confidential". It is advisable that a non-confidential summary or version of confidential documents is prepared and attached to the file.

Content of the notification form

The notification should include:

- the type of merger; and
- the following data regarding the companies participating in a merger:
  ○ the name of the company;
  ○ the place of activity;
  ○ the type of activity;
  ○ turnover in the domestic and international market;
  ○ existing market size for each of the companies, showing the methodology used for assessment and evaluation;
  ○ the size of the new participation in each company from the purchase and the total participation in the company in cases where the shares of another company are purchased; and
  ○ the name of the person authorized to represent the company.

The following documents must be attached to the notification:

- copies of the final or latest versions of all the documents regarding the concentration executed through an agreement between the parties of a concentration, acquisition of control or a public offer;
- in the case of a public offering, a copy of the document of the offer. If not available at the time of notification, it should be provided as soon as possible and no later then the time that it is sent to the shareholders;
- copies of the latest reports and annual accounts of all the parties in the concentration;
- when it has been identified of an affected market:
  - copies of the analysis, studies and surveys being prepared or sent to a board member, supervisory board or the general meeting of the shareholders for the purpose of evaluating or analysing the concentration in respect of competition, competitors and market conditions.

The company may be required by the Competition Authority to submit other relevant documentation. The notification should be signed by the authorized representative of the company.

Following the provisions of the Regulation on Competition, the notification form is provided when the fee of $150 is paid to the Authority.

Investigative procedures and sanctions

An investigation can be opened by the Competition Authority on the basis of a formal complaint by the Assembly or by regulatory institutions of specific sectors, or it may conduct a general inquiry into that sector through its own initiative, eg. if in any sector of the economy the rigidity of prices or other circumstances suggest that competition is being restricted or distorted in the market.

Further, the law provides for the right of the Competition Authority to enter into premises during an investigative procedure, to examine documents that can be accepted as evidence in proceedings, compel representatives or members of staff of the undertaking to testify, or require sanctions to be imposed for the delayed or incomplete provision of relevant documents by the entity being investigated. The Secretariat investigators must have prior authorization by way of a decision of the Commission to start investigation procedures as provided by the law.

In general, the sanctions provided for in cases where entities infringe the legislation include:

- fines;
- obligations to act or refrain from acting in a certain manner prescribed by the Commission;
- the interruption of contractual relationships;
- the ordering of concerned entities to take the necessary steps to restore their previous position;

- in particular the separation of merged entities;
- withdrawal from participating in the concentration or agreement or from the acquisition; and
- any other remedy enabling the elimination of anti-competitive behaviour.

The Authority shall give the undertaking the opportunity to participate in the process of determining penalties and obligations. In fixing the amount of the fine, regard shall be had both to the gravity and to the duration of the infringement. Where it is possible to calculate or estimate objectively the illegal profits acquired as a result of infringing this law, such profit constitutes the minimum amount of the fine.

Infringements

The Law provides several categories of infringement. In the case of those which are determined to be minor infringements, a fine will be imposed that varies between 0 and 1 per cent of the total turnover in the preceding business year.

For serious infringements, fines that vary between 2 and 10 per cent of the total turnover in the previous fiscal year will be imposed and may additionally be imposed on each participant. The latter category will generally be for horizontal restrictions, eg cartels, which are aimed at fixing prices, production or sales quotas, sharing, and any other trading conditions, or other practices that jeopardize the proper functioning of the market. They might also include an abuse of a dominant position (refusals to supply, discrimination, exclusion, loyalty discounts) made by dominant firms in order to shut competitors out of the market.

The Law also provides for a list of other administrative violations, which include infringements that disregard decisions of the Commission. In such cases, fines in periodic payments of up to 5 per cent of the average daily turnover in the preceding business year will be imposed.

No criminal responsibility can be imposed for violation of Albanian competition law.

The Law provides for a significant element of judicial remedy. Parties who have suffered loss through anti-competitive behaviour of a particular entity can ask for compensation against that entity by filing a lawsuit with the civil chamber of Tirana District Court. The right to seek a judicial remedy is in addition to the usual administrative procedures before the Competition Authority, and such judicial procedures can run independently of any administrative procedure initiated by the Competition Authority. In any event, requests for exemption from the prohibition of an agreement and the procedures on control of concentrations are not within the jurisdiction of the courts. Based on the investigation results provided by the Secretariat, the Commission can determine appropriate decisions, which can be appealed within 30 days of the notification of the decision to the administrative section of Tirana District Court. There are also determined provisions relating to leniency. Total or partial relief from financial penalties may be granted to an undertaking that, together with others, engaged in a practice prohibited by the provisions of the Law, but helped establish the reality of the existence of the prohibited practice and identify the perpetrators by providing information not previously available to the Competition Authority. The Competition Law also provides for cooperation between the Competition Authority and other institutions. This cooperation includes:

- exchange of information with corresponding foreign authorities;
- suspension or termination of proceedings in cooperation with other authorities;
- the nature of the relationship with other regulatory authorities; and
- provision for other bodies to seek the Competition Authority's opinion on any pertinent issues.

The success of implementation lies not solely with the Competition Authority, but also with the government, the courts and other regulatory institutions and with private agencies whose willingness to cooperate in implementation is essential.

2.11

Import-Export Regulations

Kalo & Associates

The main aim of the Albanian legislature is to operate to European Union (EU) standards and the creation of an appropriate environment for the development of trade. Despite the considerable improvements made in recent years, however, the harmonization of the Albanian legal framework with that of EU legislation remains a very sensitive and challenging issue.

Both import and export have grown rapidly in recent years, with the EU being Albania's main trading partner. In 2005, the EU received 88 per cent of all Albanian exports and supplied 62 per cent of all imports into Albania. Within the EU, Italy and Greece are Albania's biggest and most prominent trading partners, accounting for 83 per cent of all exports and 48 per cent of imports. Trade between the South Eastern European (SEE) countries is now increasing following the introduction of bilateral Free Trade Agreements (FTAs).

Since Albania's entry into the World Trade Organization (WTO) in 2000, the country has significantly reduced its trade-weighted average import tariff from 15.3 per cent in 1998 to 11 per cent in 2000, to 8.2 per cent in 2005. The real trade-weighted average tariff in Albania is even lower if the effects of imports from various countries having a privileged trade status (through bilateral FTAs) are taken in account.

Albania signed a Stabilization Association Agreement (SAA) with the EU in Luxembourg on 12 June 2006. This has been an important motivating factor for Albania in its struggle to amend its legislation in order to harmonize it with that of the EU and to open its market to regional and European producers. Pursuant to the Interim Agreement signed 1 December 2006, which is enforceable and in place pending the ratification of the SAA, industrial products originating from Albania will be exported into the EU with a 0 per cent customs tariff, while 83 per cent of industrial goods originating in the EU can be imported into Albania without any custom tariffs. The customs tariff that affects the remaining 17 per cent of industrial products originating in the EU will be lifted within a period of five years.

FTAs with SEE countries are based upon the principle of reciprocity and mutual advantage. The purpose is to substantially reduce and liberalize customs, duties and other trade barriers, and above all, to eliminate the discrimination in bilateral and multilateral trade relations between the signatory countries. FTAs provide for the establishment of free trade areas between the signatory countries over a period of five to six years through the elimination of the tariffs on trade. These agreements differentiate between industrial and agricultural goods. Total or partial protection over agricultural goods remains, while industrial products, with few exceptions, are subject to progressive tariff reduction. Presently, Albania has in place FTAs with Bosnia and Herzegovina, Bulgaria, Croatia, Kosovo, FYR Macedonia, Romania, Serbia, Montenegro, Moldova and Turkey. In addition, the Albanian government has expressed its will to participate in a new free trade initiative in the region.

Sources of law

The primary pieces of legislation regulating import-export are:

* Customs Code (1999);
* Law on Antidumping and Counter-Balancing Measures (2007);
* Law on the Refining, Transport and Trade of the Oil, Natural Gas and Their Sub Products (1999);
* Law on the Creation of the Agency for Stimulation of the Exports (2003);
* Law on the Nomenclature of the Goods and Custom Tariffs (2005);
* Law on Joining the 1971 United Nations Convention for Psychotropic Substances (2002);
* Law on Food (2008);
* Law on the Veterinarian Service and Inspectorate (2004);
* Mineral Law (1994);
* Law on Joining the 1975 Convention on International Trade of Endangered Species of Wild Fauna and Flora (2003);
* Law on Medicines and Pharmaceutical Service (2004);
* Law on State Import-Export Control of Military Goods and Dual-Use Goods and Technologies (2007).

There is no single law purely dedicated to the regulation of import and export (aside from the Customs Code), and each of the laws mentioned above contains specific provisions to regulate import and export within the context of its scope. There is also further secondary legislation that provides further regulation of import and export activities.

Customs regime

Over the last decade, the customs regime has been modernized with the assistance of the EU and important steps have been taken towards achieving

EU and WTO standards. These have also allowed the country to effect the various FTAs signed by the Albanian government.

The Custom Code provides for different regimes for the circulation of goods within Albania. Customs regimes require authorization from the authorities, which usually requires the applicant to provide guarantees for the payment of any customs duties and confirmation that the authorities will continue to be able to survey the goods. Treatment under a customs regime will terminate upon the assignment of the goods to another destination or the placement of the goods under another regime by the authorities. Below is a general overview of the main customs regimes in place.

Free circulation

This allows the import or release of goods into free circulation within the territory of Albania. Goods set under this regime are subject to all trade policy measures, such as customs duties and other related payments. Value-added tax (VAT) on imports is paid at the time the goods enter the Albanian customs territory.

Temporary permit

Non-Albanian goods that are imported and that are to remain for a certain period of time within the territory, and thereafter exported, can remain in the Albanian customs territory completely or partially exempt from import duties and any trade policy measures, provided that the goods have not been altered (except for depreciation in value). The maximum period that goods can be held under this regime is one year; after this period they must be exported. The amount of customs duties payable in this case is 3 per cent of the total duties that would be paid for these goods if they were subject to full customs duties.

Processing under customs control

This allows goods to be imported from outside Albania for processing operations, changing the nature or status of the goods, without their being subject to import duties or other trade policy measures. Duty becomes payable when the finished product is put into free circulation, as if it had been imported directly in order to be put into free circulation.

Active processing

This covers mainly foreign goods that are subject to amendment or transformation (to be assembled, etc.) within Albanian customs territory.

Such goods are not subject to import duties or trade limitations, and reimbursement is permitted only if import duties were paid when the goods were set into free circulation. The final goods must be exported after processing. The goods must meet a processing measurement set by the authorities, and authorization for processing commercial goods will only be issued when the subjects are established in Albania, the imported goods are recognizable within the final goods, and the interests of Albanian producers are protected.

Passive processing

This permits Albanian products to be temporarily exported for further processing outside the country and to be brought back into Albania subject to total or partial exemption of import duties. The relevant authorities will authorize the application of this regime upon request, however, only if it is possible to identify the originally exported goods within the final imported goods, and such is not contrary to the interests of local producers. There are also some other restrictions.

Temporary warehouse

Under this regime, goods and products are permitted to be stored for a specific period in certain customs storage warehouses that are approved by the relevant authority. During this period they will not be subject to any customs duties. The storage period is 12 months with the possibility of an extension for a further 12 months.

Transit

This regime covers the movement of non-Albanian goods and/or vehicles that pass through the territory of Albania on their way to another country. Such goods transiting the territory of Albania are exempt from customs duty, VAT and excise taxes. Evidence must be shown to the customs authorities that the goods do not originate from Albania and are only passing through the country.

Export

This is applied to all Albanian products destined to be exported outside the Albanian customs territory. Exports are exempt from VAT, and persons/companies exporting can benefit from a VAT credit for purchases made in respect of the products to be exported.

Licensing and sanctions for the import-export of special goods

Albanian legislation provides for special import-export licences for those goods for which the usually accepted guarantee of their origination/ production is not sufficient for the regulation of their import-export. Specific import-export licences, subject to the fulfilment of special technical requirements, are required for the import or export of oil, natural gas and their sub products. Specific licences and authorizations are also required for the import-export of chemical materials, and for the import of military goods and technologies. The provisions relating to the latter were enacted in the Law on State Import-Export Control of Military Goods and Dual-Use Goods and Technologies, and such provisions are required as a pre-condition for Albania's entrance to NATO.

Trade of oil, gas and sub products

By the very nature of the pre-conditions for acquiring a licence in this field typically only large companies trade in this field. The licence for these companies is subject to the fulfilment of special technical and commercial conditions. For example, such companies should be in the form of a joint-stock company, have a specific required storage capacity, a reserve for a specified period of oil/gas, etc. These companies must be capable of maintaining a continuous supply in their plants and to guarantee a continuous supply to their contractors. As provided in the legislation, such companies have the right to create or to be participants in companies that have as their object a detailed trading activity, eg. the establishing and running of a petrol/gas station.

Trade of chemical materials

Pursuant to the legislation regulating this area, the import-export of chemicals is only permitted with a special licence from the relevant state authority, and the ministry of the environment is authorized to check the registers or e-lines of chemicals that are imported in Albania. Such licence and approval must be sought no later that 60 days before the day on which the materials will be imported or exported. The office for the registration of the chemical materials registers the application for the import-export licences and notifies the ministry of the environment.

The ministry of the environment approves the list of dangerous chemicals that are permitted to be distributed, and those for which the usage is to be limited or prohibited in the market. Presently, the licences set out and specify the period for the validity of the licence and the quantity permitted to be imported/exported within that period of validity.

Import-export of military goods and dual-use technologies

The official body for issuing licences for the trade of these goods is the State Authority of Export Control. There are two types of licence, namely those valid for specific purposes and those valid for general purposes. The conditions for the issue of the unlimited general licences are the creation of the intra-organized system of the control of exports, eg. the fulfilment of the necessary requirements as prescribed by the law and the State Authority of Export Control, the preservation of the due documentation related to these transfers and the presentation of relevant reports to the State Authority of Export Control.

The time periods for the consideration of the applications, according to the law, are:

- 45 days for the export of military goods;
- 30 days for the export of dual-use goods (ie. for both military and non-military use) and the temporary import-export of these materials; and
- 15 days for the import or the transiting or temporary import-export of materials for exposition, publicity and similar purposes, should the import-export not impose a change of ownership.

The State Authority of Export Control is responsible for issuing licences and authorizations or international certificates of import. The documents submitted by applicants should contain accurate data on the materials and the procedures of the international transfer, and the original guarantees for these transfers. Upon refusal to grant a licence, the State Authority of Export Control is required to include the reasons for such refusal.

There are specific sanctions provided by the law that include the revoking of a licence/authorization in the case of violation of legislation, including the violation of transport legislation. There are further sanctions provided for, eg. within the Albanian Penal Code.

The following are considered violations of the State Authority of Export Control rules on import-export:

- international transfer of equipment without the proper licence and required state guarantee;
- international transfer of equipment based on licences procured with incorrect or manipulated documentation;
- procurement of international contracts for the transfer of equipment where the subject involved in the transfer has received information that the equipment will be used by the foreign subject or country for the creation of weapons of mass destruction;
- distortion of the final destination of the equipment in international transfers as set out in the declaration of the contract according to which

the licence for import-export has been issued, or even the distortion of the specified use or of the final beneficiary;

- intentional non-disclosure of important information;
- international transfer of equipment in violation of the conditions provided for in the licence, including distortion of the contract conditions without permission from the State Authority of Export Control;
- negotiation of contracts for the export of military goods or dual-use equipment to a country partially under embargo, without permission from the State Authority of Export Control;
- obstructing the State Authority of Export Control or other state bodies in the official exercise of their duties;
- unjustifiable and unreasonable refusal to provide information or documents required by the State Authority of Export Control or any other state body; and
- intentional destruction of documents related to the procurement or implementation of agreements/contracts for the international transfer of equipment, according to which the licences have been issued.

The law authorizes the State Authority of Export Control to apply penalties to those subjects that are in violation of its provisions.

Import-export of psychotropic substances

Psychotropic substances are another class of materials for which Albanian law provides special trade and production licences. Interested parties in the import-export of these materials must make an application to acquire a specific licence. In its application, the party should specify the nature of the activity, the countries in which the activity will be exercised and the names of the substances that are the object of the activity. The licence issued by the authority contains the duration of its validity, the type of substances related to the authorized activity, their quantity and other terms and conditions that the holder of the licence should fulfil. The licence issued by the authorities cannot be transferred to third parties.

The licence can be revoked where the provisions of the respective law are violated. This includes irregularities in the exercise of the authorized activity, especially violations of the terms and conditions specified in the actual licence, where the responsible personnel have proved not to be sufficiently cautious, or in the case that incorrect information was given at the time of the licence. For less serious violations, the ministry of health may suspend the licence for a period of up to six months. The suspension of the licence can be followed by further penal or administrative sanctions as provided by other laws.

2.12

Privatization Law

Përparim Kalo, Managing Partner, Kalo & Associates

Introduction

New concepts of privatization were introduced in Albania immediately after the end of communism in 1990. The first pluralistic parliament in nearly half a century enacted the earliest bills to encourage private initiatives and, at the same time, lifted the prohibition on foreign capital entering the Albanian market, thus exposing the state-owned enterprises to privatization. It was a big step forward, given the fact that the Albanian economy was strictly centralized and the Constitution had prohibited foreign capital from flowing in since 1946.

Legal framework

The first bill on privatization was introduced in 1990, and it was approved and enacted in the following year as the Law on the Sanctioning and Protection of Private Property, Free Initiative, Independent Private Activities and Privatization (No. 7512, 10 August 1991). This law:

- recognized private property rights in general and introduced the idea of privatization of state enterprises in particular;
- set out the framework for the full restitution of nationalized properties to the original owners;
- enabled both local and foreign investors to start private businesses;
- provided legal guarantees for the protection of investors; and
- created the basis for building a legal framework that would regulate specific sectors of the economy.

Other pieces of subsidiary legislation provided further detail for the institutions in charge of privatization, their role and tasks and also the relevant procedures to be followed.

Within a short period of time, several further laws were enacted to foster the process of privatization, among which two are considered as the cornerstone of the very first phase of the course of privatization: the Company

Law (1992) and the Law on Foreign Investment (1993). While the Company Law, aside from providing the legal basis and framework for private business structures, sets out the rationale and provided the necessary tools to facilitate foreign investments in Albania, the Law on Foreign Investment abolished or minimized heavy bureaucratic barriers, recognized the right to select foreign laws for dispute resolution in international commercial agreements and guaranteed the right to freely repatriate funds overseas, etc.

In the subsequent years, numerous laws were enacted to address the issues that needed to be regulated in order to support the new concept of private business, which in turn was also required to support the process of privatization. Some of laws that ensued are as follows:

- Law on Land (1991);
- Law on Restitution and Compensation of Properties to Ex-Owners (1993), now repealed by a new one in 2004;
- Law on Sale and Purchase of Construction Land (1995);
- Law on Competition (1995, now replaced by the new 2003 Law on Competition Protection);
- Law on Concessions (1995, later replaced by the new 2006 Law on Concessions);
- Law on Companies (1992), being reconsidered;
- Law on Mining (1994), being reconsidered;
- Law on Income Tax (1993, repealed in 1998);
- Law on Banks (1992, repealed in 1998 and a new one enacted in 2006);
- Law on Telecommunications (1995, repealed by Law No. 8618, 14 June 2000);
- Law on Regulation of the Electric Energy Sector (1995); and
- Law on Water Reserves (1996).

Initially, the majority of small enterprises were privatized, but what remained were, in the main, medium and large state-owned enterprises that necessitated a distinctive privatization strategy. In this regard the Law on Transformation of State-Owned Enterprises into Commercial Companies and a Presidential Decree 'On Issuing and the Distribution of Privatization Vouchers' were enacted in 1995. The Law set up the National Privatization Agency as the central institution responsible for the transformation of state-owned enterprises into commercial companies. The provision of privatization vouchers was an incentive to the public that had contributed to the public, and indeed only, sector in Albania. Furthermore, after the incorporation of those state-owned entities, rules and procedures for the privatization of their shares or assets were enacted. Another important piece of legislation connected with the privatization process was the Law on the Restitution of Properties to Former Owners (1993), later replaced by a new law (No. 9235, dated 2004, and amended in 2006), which clearly stipulated the right of former owners to regain their properties. Amongst other provisions, this law also provided for the participation of former owners in the privatization of assets or shares of companies by converting their property rights into assets or shares.

New efforts were made from time to time to introduce new legislation, and also to replace the then existing laws where necessary to emulate the experiences of other countries. Hence the Law on Sanctioning and Protecting Private Property, Free Initiative, Independent Private Activities and Privatization (No. 7512) was first amended in 1995, and then again in 1998, when the new set of privatization laws replaced the general framework.

However, past experience of privatization had brought about several uncertainties mainly because privatization procedures were launched and implemented by resolutions of the Council of Ministers. New legislation was enacted in 1998 to specifically regulate privatization procedures by law: (i) a law governing the privatization of state-owned companies operating in strategic sectors such as banking, insurance, water, airports, ports, telecommunications, power, etc., and (ii) a law governing the privatization of state-owned companies operating in other secondary sectors.

Although these later laws re-established the legal framework for privatization and provided general rules, the privatization of each individual company was initiated only upon the enactment of a specific law, which would establish the form and formula of the privatization. The formula has varied on a case-by-case basis, although some of the important elements of the privatization process have been consistently repeated. In many cases, the laws have consistently addressed:

- the right of the state to retain a "golden share";
- the property rights of former owners of a company's assets;
- the right of employees (or families) to exchange shares for privatization vouchers; and
- the compensation, in the case of collective redundancy as a result of the privatization.

Even the specific laws tend to set out the general provision, allowing for negotiation of the finer details that will be encompassed in secondary legislation and in the transaction documents. In most cases, if not all, the privatizations of state-owned companies undergo either a tender procedure or an auction. Auction has normally been used when the State of Albania did not have any interest in keeping those activities under its control and simply sold the enterprise to generate cash. Conversely, the tender procedure has been utilized to ensure that the business activity and the ownership of the assets are managed and owned by specialized operators.

Privatization of state-owned enterprises

In 1995, the ministry of finance, the National Agency of Privatization and the Bank of Albania launched a "Voucher Privatization" programme, better known as the Mass Privatization Programme. Vouchers were distributed to all Albanians over 18 years of age (as of 1992) and were divided into three age groups and several phases. The Bank of Albania was responsible for printing the vouchers and the Savings Bank for distributing them to eligible recipients. The programme also required state-owned enterprises to transform into joint-stock companies according to a specific law of 1995, prior to their privatization through the sale of shares.

In the Mass Privatization Programme, voucher holders had the choice of investing their vouchers in investment funds, established as joint-stock companies.

From the very beginning, there was a low level of demand for vouchers, given the fact that the process of privatization of assets scheduled for privatization was delayed or in some cases the assets were not considered economically profitable. Prices of vouchers remained at relatively low levels and the whole idea faded away due to:

(a)   a lack of vision in the privatization process;
(b)   weaknesses in the privatization process;
(c)   a miscalculation of the total amount of vouchers to be distributed to the population;
(d)   delays in offering the necessary assets for voucher privatization; and
(e)   the consequences of the collapse of pyramid schemes in 1997.

Consequently, today, the market of vouchers almost does not exist in the sense originally intended, and this has led to a dispersed post-privatization ownership structure that assumes that the transfer of significant ownership stakes to single parties may have greater efficiency gains than privatization that disperses ownership.

The second phase of privatization sought to improve the activities of governmental structures aimed at administering government funds. In addition, the second phase was meant to further the liberalization and coherence of the market, in line with the macroeconomic development of the country. The new privatization programme, aimed at transferring ownership of special strategic sectors of the Albanian economy, including oil and gas, electric power, telecommunication, transport infrastructure and water infrastructure, had to be achieved in close relation with strategic investors, to whom ownership of a significant portion of the share capital was to be transferred.

Privatization of strategic sectors

The privatization of enterprises operating in strategic sectors is governed in accordance with the overall Privatization Strategy, approved by the Law on the Strategy of Privatization of Companies Operating in Primary Sectors (No. 8306, 14 March 1998), and is headed by the Consultancy and

Transparency Committee, set up by Council of Ministers Decree (DCM) On the Creation of Consultancy and Transparency Committee for Privatizing Sectors of Special Importance (DCM No. 621, 25 September 1998, later amended by DCM No. 32, 28 January 2002). This plan enabled the government to divest state shares in joint ventures to private sector counterparts and private enterprises in strategic sectors. Furthermore, the privatization strategy provided that publicly owned businesses could be sold below book value, which, in many cases, did not reflect the market value.

This new approach indicated important changes in the economic, social and political reform that was to have an essential and positive impact on the Albanian market. A sector strategy was elaborated and coordinated in direct cooperation with the Council of Ministers, individual ministries and the competent regulatory bodies to establish the conditions and guarantee the fulfilment of the privatization programme.

The programme to privatize the most important sectors of the economy aimed at the sale of at least 75 per cent of state-owned assets. Some of the strategic sectors mentioned above still face tough challenges due to:

- old technology and a bad overall technical situation, owing to the lack of investment over an extended period of time;
- inferior management and inadequate planning;
- strong intervention by the state in daily activities;
- insufficient knowledge of market rules, a low level of financial discipline, and a low level of checks and balances; and
- conflicting or vague objectives under political patronage, hampering efficiency.

For these reasons, a large portion was offered to strategic investors with a view to them injecting their experience, skill and capital into the business, in order to ultimately provide a better service to the public and, of course, to permit the investor to generate some profits.

The Law on the Strategy of Privatization of Companies Operating in Primary Sectors opened up to privatization all companies with state-owned capital that operated in strategic sectors and played or had the potential to play a significant role in the country's economy, such as telecommunications, ports, mines, power, oil and gas, forests, water, infrastructure, insurance and banks with state-owned capital.

According to the procedures defined by this law, a further specific law was to be approved to address issues arising from the privatization of each public company. For example, the Law on Privatization of Anonymous Albanian Mobile Communications Companies (AMC) (No. 8515, 21 July 1999) and the Law on the Definition of the Privatization Structure and Formula of Anonymous Company Albtelecom (No. 8810, 17 May 2001) were approved exclusively to deal with those privatizations. However, in any single case, it was required that the Council of Ministers should approve by specific resolutions the following issues:

- procedures of tender for the selection of strategic investors and the transfer of shares;
- the criteria for the selection of strategic investors interested in buying shares;
- the criteria for evaluating bids on the privatization of companies operating in strategic sectors;
- allocation of income generated by the privatization of the company;
- draft of share purchase contract and instructions for the submission and opening of bids for the privatization of strategic sector companies; and
- report of evaluation of bids for the privatization of the company.

Financial services

In the financial sector, some restrictions have continuously influenced the lack of interest from strategic investors. For example, in insurance, a foreign investor could hold only 40 per cent of the shares in an insurance company. This restriction, which discouraged investors, was maintained until 2000. Privatization in the insurance industry started with the transfer of 39 per cent of Albania's insurance company, INSIG, to the International Finance Corporation (IFC) and the European Bank for Reconstruction and Development (EBRD). The IFC and EBRD had INSIG under their supervision for a transitional period of one to two years, thus giving way to the attraction of strategic investors and the sale of the majority of shares. Now a privatization advisor has been selected by the government and privatization of the remaining shares is expected to be completed by the end of 2008.

The first stage of the banking privatization process started with the Decree on Accelerating the Process of Privatization of Commercial Banks with State-Owned Capital (No. 1648, 20 November 1996). This decree brought to an end unprofitable banking activities and promoted the acceleration of the privatization process by requiring the necessary amendments to the existing state-owned banking network and the respective organizational structures. The second wave of privatization was successful and 100 per cent of the Savings Bank's shares were transferred to Raiffeisen Bank in January 2004. Subsequently, state-owned shares in the joint venture Italian-Albanian Bank were transferred to San Paolo Intesa Group. Since the opening of the banking market, the Albanian banking sector now has 18 privately owned banks.

Confidence in the banking sector appears to have increased with local and foreign deposits both growing since 2003. Despite the positive impact of the privatization of the Savings Bank, the financial sector still needs to strengthen its structures, including banking supervision, and to play a more central role in the country's economic development (particularly by being more active in providing credit to productive units). Efforts have been made to reduce the volume of cash transactions and to promote the use of the banking sector, notably through steps towards the payment of civil servants' salaries through the banks, and encouragement to pay electricity and telephone bills through the banks.

With regard to the Tirana Stock Exchange, the definitive licence to operate in the country's capital market has been issued. The Tirana Stock Exchange is intended to serve as a secondary market of the government's treasury bills and obligations, and for the listing and trading of shares and obligations of Albanian companies. Unfortunately, the stock exchange has yet to function in reality.

Telecommunications

In 1999, the Albanian government concluded a $85.6 million privatization agreement with the Norwegian company Telenor International, and Greece's Cosmote for the country's first mobile network, while in 2001, it awarded the second GSM licence to Vodafone with the highest bid of $38 million through an international tender.

The privatization of the Albanian telecommunications company Albtelecom faced serious problems in its early stages and the process had to be postponed due to a lack of interest from international potential bidders. Although Albtelecom was successfully sold to a Turkish industrial group, it was only after the state issued a mobile licence to a subsidiary fully owned by Albtelecom to make the company more attractive for prospective buyers.

Mining and oil

For the privatization of the mining sector, a law established the sector's division into large, medium and small enterprises. The largest enterprises have been privatized, allowing strategic investors to hold not less than 30 per cent of shares, whereas, conversely, shares of medium-sized companies have been sold to strategic or non-strategic investors. Small enterprises have been privatized by joint-stock or limited liability companies by giving priority privatization securities.

The situation is somewhat more advanced in the oil sector, as the privatizations of Albpetrol (production), ARMO (refinery) and Servcom (distribution) are in the process of evaluation.

Energy

The energy sector is also open to privatization, in particular the electrical energy sector. In this regard, the production and distribution activities of electric power plants are subject to privatization in parallel with the promotion of new private investments in the entire energy sector. Privatization of production and distribution will be done by incorporating the relevant assets of these activities into a joint-stock company of which a large part of its share capital will be offered to strategic investors. The privatization of the distribution division of the state-owned company, Albanian Power Corporation (KESH), is already under way. The distribution division has almost been unbundled as a distinct joint-stock company with its own assets, liabilities, etc, in order to be offered to strategic investors. This is one of the largest privatization deals in the country at present and is very much at the heart of the interest of the government, in light of the serious electricity shortages in the country.

It is expected that the strategic sector will be offered a controlling package of the unbundled distribution company, with some expectation of injection of capital, skill and experience to make the company a much more efficient and profit-making service.

Social problems

Key to the development and implementation of the country's privatization strategy and efficient policies for market liberalization was finding an appropriate resolution to socio-economic conflicts and maintaining the pace of recapitalization of the economy in accordance with the socio-economic situation.

As mentioned above, the specific laws relating to the privatization of specific state enterprises provide provisions as to how to deal with employees (ie. both those who are made redundant and those who remain with the company after privatization), and also how to deal with former land owners of the property that is to be privatized. These are the two issues that are considered to be the related "social problems" that, according to the laws on privatization, must be resolved.

Employees

With the privatization of enterprises within strategic sectors, the government provides not only for those employees who will be made redundant as a result of the privatization but also for those who will remain with the company after privatization. The specific laws on the privatization of an actual company usually provide for a small percentage (usually not more than 5 per cent) of the share capital to be offered to employees (or families of the employee) in exchange for privatization vouchers. This provision is not strictly an employee incentive provision but seems also to be a way of utilizing all those privatization vouchers issued by the government in 1995. It may be the case that not all employees have such vouchers available, though it is likely that if they do not then their spouse or parents will.

More important is to deal with those employees who are made redundant as a result of privatization. State enterprises subject to privatization were often overstaffed, and probably with staff that the private investor would deem not sufficiently experienced. This is obviously a politically sensitive issue, particularly where large numbers of people are required to be dismissed. Although the Labour Code provides for redundancy-type compensation, the government tends to provide more generous compensation. For example, in the case of Albtelecom, pursuant to the Decision on the Treatment of the Employees that Remain Jobless after the Process of Albtelecom Restructuring (No. 495 of 14 August 2001), redundant employees were offered a two-year remuneration package at 100 per cent of their net salary at the moment of redundancy. This was offered to employees having at least two years of seniority and unless and until they found another job. The costs were covered by Albtelecom before the finalization of the privatization process and from the privatization revenues after it.

Former land owners

Pursuant to the State Property Law (No. 8743, 22 February 2001), state-owned immovable properties can be:

* public property (state-owned immovable property "which performs fundamental and inseparable state functions and brings benefit to the public"); and
* non-public state-owned immovable property.

Restitution and compensation in Albania is regulated essentially by the Law on Restitution and Compensation of Property (No. 9235, 29 July 2004), as amended. This Restitution Law provides that subjects that were expropriated after 1944 have the right to request ownership rights and restitution or compensation of the property. Compensation is defined as just remuneration according to the market value of the property at the moment this remuneration is recognized. In the light of the focus here on strategic sectors, it should be noted that under this Law on Restitution, immovable property that serves a public interest and is occupied inter alia on the basis of a specific Privatization and Investment Law is not subject to restitution, but to compensation.

In the specific privatization laws enacted, the government tends to offer, as with employees, a specific percentage of shares to cover "fair compensation" for former owners of property that remains with a privatized company that will serve a public service.

Concessions

"Privatization" is defined broadly in the law on the privatization of strategic sectors and includes various forms of private sector participation, such as concessions and long-term leases. Concessions are defined as agreements between a contracting authority and a concessionaire whereby the latter provides an economic activity that would otherwise be carried out by the contracting authority, which assumes all or a substantial part of the risk related to such activity and receives a benefit by direct payment paid by or on behalf of the contracting authority, user tariffs or fees or a combination thereof.

Concessions have been used as a mode of privatization for large state enterprises within the strategic sector of airports and are typically used for the rehabilitation, design and building of power plants, water sewage treatment systems, road sectors and also ports. Albania is utilizing all available forms of public-private partnerships in a bid to improve public services and develop the market economy.

The future of strategic privatizations

The privatization programme in Albania includes all important sectors of the economy, such as oil and gas, electric power, telecommunication, transport infrastructure and water infrastructure. Its realization requires the coordination of detailed programmes with line ministries, the coordination of activities for the development of sector policies and the introduction of a clear and strong regulatory framework for each sector.

The privatization of state-owned companies operating in strategic sectors can be considered as a successful undertaking of the Albanian government. However, it is important to highlight some of the challenges that the persons in charge of this activity have to consider in the future:

1. a definition and understanding of the impact that a privatization is expected to give to the specific industry. Privatization has often been seen as a simple transfer of ownership rather than a quality change. In other words, institutional strengthening is required prior to privatization for end-consumers to receive quality services;
2. the creation of a capital market that would maximize the sale proceeds to be received in a privatization. It is a known fact that the capital market failed to develop, even though a securities law was enacted in 1996;
3. institutional strengthening of the companies that are to be privatized in the restructuring phase to maximize price, but also to prepare the privatized company for survival against likely competition in its specific industry;
4. the creation of market rules simultaneously with privatization so that companies resulting from privatization do not create monopolies or oligopolies. This will require the state to play a role as regulator of industries and not to be considered simply as a seller that just sells and does not care about the future of the privatized industry.

2.13

Intellectual Property Law

Shirli Gorenca, Associate, Kalo & Associates

Introduction

Although many intellectual property (IP) rights are territorially based, they have always had a strong international dimension. European Community law has had a positive impact on IP rights in Albania and has prompted many changes.

The previous Law on Industrial Property (No. 7819), 1994, as amended in 1999, is soon to be abrogated with the introduction of the new Law on Industrial Property (No. 9947), 2008, which is to come into effect in November 2008. This new law has been prompted by new market requirements, as the protection of patents and trademarks is increasingly recognized as a key business requirement. In general, Albania's legal system complies with international standards on mutual recognition of IP rights.

The forms of IP protection available in the Republic of Albania are as follows:

- trademarks and service marks;
- industrial designs;
- geographical indications;
- inventions and utility models (protected by patents); and
- copyrights (provided for in a separate Law on Copyrights, 2005, as amended in 2008).

Trademarks, industrial designs and geographical indications

Trademarks

A trademark is a symbol, either in the form of a word, letter, slogan, design, shape or appearance of packaging, or any other symbol that identifies and distinguishes a product or service. The purpose of the trademark is to enable the customers to recognize a product, thus enabling them to rely on a given trademark to tell them that a product is of a consistent level of quality to which they are accustomed.

To be eligible for registration, however, a trademark must be capable of distinguishing the goods or services of one trader from those of another. For this reason, a trademark should not consist of:

- elements or indications that are used to indicate the kind, quality, quantity, purpose, value, geographical origin, or time of production of the goods or services, or any other such indication of their characteristics;
- elements or indications that are common in ordinary language, or that are turned into trade practices;
- shapes or lines imposed by the nature of the goods or services;
- geographical indications for wines and spirits that do not originate from the countries indicated in those geographical indications;
- marks comprising the emblems, names, flags and symbols of international organizations of which Albania is a member, unless authorized. The following would be prohibited from registration:
  o Red Cross;
  o Geneva Cross;
  o Crescent; Red Crescent;
  o the abbreviations UNESCO and NATO; and
  o the words United Nations;
- state, national and regional flags, or state names (complete or abbreviated);
- state emblems, abbreviations and emblems of intergovernmental organizations, or official hallmarks adopted by states;
- religious symbols;
- surnames, portraits, pseudonyms of persons well known (by the general public) without authorization of the owner thereof or their successors in title; and
- signs that violate public order or morality, etc.

Trademark protection

In essence, registering a trademark gives the owner the right to prevent others from "infringing", i.e. using the mark in such a way that is likely to cause confusion to the customers as to the source of the product. Trademarks may be registered with the General Directorate of Patents and Trademarks (GDPT). The steps involved are as follows:

1. Decide whether national or international protection is going to be sought.
2. Make a preliminary search to find out if any identical or similar trademarks have already been registered in Albania, or have been applied for an international registration.

3. Provided that the search results in there being no identical or similar trademarks already registered, the application for registration can be proceeded with.

The trademark protection (for a period of 10 years) begins from the date of filing the application. Just prior to the expiration of the 10-year period, it is advisable to submit an application for renewal of the trademark registration to avoid gaps in protection.

Within five months from the date of filing an application, the GDPT shall publish its decision on the trademark registration.

Industrial designs

Industrial designs are IP rights that protect the visual design of objects that are not purely utilitarian. An industrial design can be a two or three-dimensional pattern used to produce a product, industrial commodity or handicraft. Protection for a registered industrial design can last up to 25 years, subject to the payment of renewal fees every five years.

Under the Hague Agreement on the International Deposit of Industrial Designs, an applicant can file for a single international deposit with the World Intellectual Property Organization, or with the national office in a country party to the treaty. The design will then be protected in as many member countries of the treaty as desired.

Geographical indications

Geographical indications are names or signs used on certain products, which correspond to a specific geographical location or origin (eg. a town, region, or country). The use of a geographical indication may act as a certification that the product possesses certain qualities, or enjoys a certain reputation, due to its geographical origin.

The protection of geographical indications can last for an indefinite period of time, and it only terminates when there is no more connection between the characteristics and qualities of the good and its geographical environment.

Licence agreement

A licence agreement is any contract by which the owner of a registered trademark or industrial design (the licensor) gives to a licensee his/her agreement for the licensee to use the registered mark or industrial design. The contract should be made in writing and be signed by the parties to the contract. The licence contract shall also be recorded in the register of marks or industrial designs on payment of the prescribed fee.

The owner of a registered geographical indication cannot assign this right to another party.

Enforcement against infringement

The registered owner of a trademark, industrial design or geographical indication has the right to commence court proceedings in the District Court of Tirana, if he/she is able to show that aninfringement is taking place and is causing damage. The court may grant an injunction to prevent further infringement. Furthermore, if the owner successfully proves his case, i.e. the existence of the infringement, the court shall award damages.

Patents

A patent protects new inventions and gives the owner the exclusive right to make, use and sell the invention in the Republic of Albania. The term granted for a new patent is usually 20 years from the date on which the application for the patent is filed at the GDTP.

Having acquired the patent, the owner shall have the right to exclude others from making, using, offering for sale, or selling the invention. To maintain the registration of a patent, an annual payment should be paid to the GDPT.

An invention is eligible for patent protection if:

(a) the invention is novel: it should not form part of the "state of the art" known to the public at the date of the patent application, and this "state of the art" shall include all information made available to the public by written/oral description, use or otherwise. It shall also include the content of any patent application as filed in Albania, provided that it is subsequently published and priority is claimed;

(b) it involves an inventive step: it must be obvious to a person skilled in the relevant art; and

(c) it is industrially applicable: it can be used or made in any kind of industry, and industry shall be understood in its broadest sense and shall cover any productive activities or services and agriculture.

The following shall not be considered to be inventions when considering the above conditions:

- discoveries, scientific theories and mathematical methods;
- aesthetic creations;
- schemes, rules and methods for performing mental acts, playing games or doing business, and computers programs;
- presentations of information;

- an invention of which the publication or exploitation of such subject matter would be contrary to public policy, morality, or health and life (eg. human cloning, modification of the genetic identity sequence of human beings, embryo or animals, use of human embryos for industrial or commercial purposes, etc.);
- animal/plant varieties or processes for plant or animal production;
- the human body;
- substances obtained through internal nuclear transformations for military purposes; and
- inventions of surgical, diagnostic or therapeutic methods practised on humans/animals, which shall be regarded as inventions not susceptible of industrial application.

Only the actual inventor may apply and own the patent, which shall be granted in his/her name. However, an inventor may transfer all or part of his/her interest in the patent application or patent by an assignment. Patents may also be licensed exclusively or non-exclusively.

Registration

The application for registration should include:

- a formal request;
- the title of the invention;
- necessary data regarding the proprietor or patent attorney;
- information related to the inventor;
- a reference declaring priority (preferably between two and seven words);
- a description of the invention;
- claims about novelty; and
- figures/designs relevant to the invention.

Albanian patent registration only protects the invention within the Republic of Albania.

Amendment or correction of an application

An applicant has the right, upon his/her own initiative, to amend or correct the application up to the time when the application is decided upon, as long as payment of the prescribed fee has taken place. However, there can be no amendment or correction of the application permitted beyond what has been disclosed in the filed application.

The GDPT publishes all applications filed, and once published the applicant shall provisionally enjoy the same rights as would be enjoyed by a patent owner as from the date of its publication. The publication of the application shall be done in the manner prescribed in the regulations of the GDPT.

Examination of the application and grant of the patent

The GDPT shall examine whether the application complies with the requirements of the law and regulations of the GDPT, and thereafter decide to grant the patent subject to the payment of the prescribed fee.

Should the application not conform, or only partially conform, to the above requirements, the GDPT shall notify the applicant, specifying the discrepancies and setting a three-month period for any response or corrections. The application will be rejected if the applicant fails to correct the deficiencies indicated. The decision of the GDPT may, on payment of fee, be appealed against to the board of appeal of the GDPT within three monts. If the applicant is not satisfied with the decision of the board of appeal, he/she may appeal this decision in court, within 13 days.

As soon as the GDPT has adopted a decision on the grant of the patent, it shall publish a notification that the patent has been granted and publish the patent specification in the prescribed manner.

Enforcement against infringement

The owner of, or applicant for, a patent has the right to pursue litigation against any person that has infringed, or is infringing, the patent or the provisional protection conferred upon a published patent application. If the owner of the patent proves that an infringement has been committed, the District Court may grant an injunction to prevent further infringement and any other remedy provided for in the general law for ascertained damages.

The Law on Industrial Property specifies the measures that should be taken by the court and other responsible institutions in cases of the infringement of patents, in compliance with the Council Directive 2004/48/EC on Protection of Industrial Property Rights and provisions of the Trade-Related Aspects of Intellectual Property Rights Agreement.

Utility models

By means of a utility model, it is possible to protect a technical solution that:

- is an invention eligible for patent; and
- is novel and industrially applicable.

Utility models are registered on the basis of a specific registration principle, whereby the GDPT enters the respective utility model into the register without examining whether the subject matter complies with the criteria of novelty and creativity, ie. whether it is capable of protection. This is the main feature distinguishing it from the protection process of patents. The process is therefore much quicker, and can be useful for products that are ready for introduction into the market.

No one can produce, introduce into the market or use the technical solution protected without the consent of the registered utility model owner. As with patents, the owner of the registered utility model is authorized to grant approval for exploitation of the respective utility model object (via a licence) to other persons, or to transfer the utility model to them.

The law relating to utility models in Albania incorporates the requirements of Council Directive 98/44/EC on the Legal Protection of Biotechnological Inventions, Council Regulation No. 1768/92 Concerning the Creation of a Supplementary Protection Certificate for Medicinal Products, and Council Regulation No. 1610/96 Concerning the Creation of a Supplementary Protection Certificate for Plant Protection Products.

Copyright

Another aspect of IP legislation is the regulation and protection of copyrights. In Albania, the governing law is the Law on Copyright and Related Rights (the Copyright Law) (No. 9380), 2005 (as amended by Law No.9934 of 26 June 2008), which applies to literary, artistic or scientific works that are created, produced and exploited for commercial or other use, or transferred to another person in the Republic of Albania.

The provisions of this law apply to works in literature, art or science, computer programs, projects, musical compositions, dramatic compositions, dramatic-musicals, choreographic compositions and pantomimes, etc. Copyright on works of literature or artistic work extends throughout the life of the author, plus 70 years after his/her death, regardless of the date that the work has been legally published. In any case, the period 1968-1991 shall not be taken into consideration.

Albanian Office for Copyrights

The government established the Albanian Office for Copyrights (ACO) in April 2006. The ACO is the competent authority dealing with copyright protection in Albania; it is a legal entity, functioning under the ministry of culture, tourism, youth and sports. The ACO examines and approves/rejects each application for registration of copyright and other related rights. It decides upon all applications, registrations and amendments on copyrights. The ACO also authorizes copyright experts to act as representatives in court, based on the provisions of the Civil Procedure Code.

Who is subject to the Copyright Law

The provisions of the Copyright Law are applicable to works that:

* are not transmitted in public, and the author(s) is (are) Albanian;
* have as their author a physical person who lives in Albania and is a resident of the country;
* are shown in public in Albania, or abroad and within 30 days are shown in Albania;
* are shown for the first time by foreign authors to the public in their country, or in a third country, and are shown in Albania within 30 days;
* are of architectural nature, and constructed in the territory of Albania; and
* are presentations of artists who live in the territory of Albania, and the registered sounds are interpreted within 30 days.

The works of foreign authors are protected under the provisions of this law and ratified international treaties to which Albania is a signatory. Registration of copyright is not mandatory in order to acquire protection. However, it is advisable as in the case of infringement, the registration and the certificate issued by the ACO shall be of paramount importance in providing evidence of the ownership of copyright.

Infringement of copyright

Any person who claims that a certain action has damaged rights arising out of their copyright may begin a lawful court procedure pursuant to the Civil Procedure Code of the Republic of Albania. They have the right to claim for:

* the destruction or the neutralization of all the materials and equipments; and
* compensation for the damage afflicted.

The author (or his/her authorized representative) should present the following to the court:

* the particulars of the infringement, stating all the identified elements of remedies sought;
* all legislation relied upon in claiming the infringement in the claim; and
* a detailed description of reasons and evidence on which the claim is based.

The decision regarding destruction or neutralization shall be taken by the court after having taken into account the opinion of an expert authorized by the ACO.

Other legislation

Constitution

The Constitution of the Republic of Albania guarantees the freedom of works of art and also guarantees their protection. In brief, Article 58 of the Constitution states that every person who creates a work of art has the right to exercise his/her creative ability, intellectual or artistic, and to protect it from any infringement by other persons, from being copied, from unfair use and reproduction without permission or consent.

Civil Code

The Civil Code contains articles that regulate contractual damage in respect of infringement causing economic or moral damage.

Criminal Code

Pursuant to the Albanian Criminal Code, "publication and complete or partial use, in the name of a literary, musical, artistic or scientific work, which relates to another, is a criminal offence and punishable by a fine or a sentence of up to one year".

For the unfair reproduction of the another's work, the law provides that a "complete or partial reproduction of the literary, musical, artistic or scientific work, which belongs to another, or its use without the author's consent … is a criminal offence and is punishable by a fine".

International agreements and treaties

Albania is a member of the 1886 Berne Convention for the Protection of Literary and Artistic Works. This Convention requires member countries to provide copyright protection for works created or first published in other member countries. Albania is also a signatory to the following international conventions:

- 1961 International Convention for the Protection of Performers, Producers of Phonograms and Broadcasting, Organization (the Rome Convention); and
- 1971 Convention for the Protection of Producers of Phonograms against Unauthorized Duplication of their Phonograms (the Geneva Phonograms Convention).

In accordance with the Constitution, any international agreements and treaties that have been ratified by the Albanian parliament take precedence over domestic legislation, and must be adhered to.

2.14

Real Estate Law

Zamira Xhaferri, Head of Commercial Property Department, Kalo & Associates

Introduction

The Albanian real estate market is proving to be one of the most efficient and dynamic of domestic economic sectors, which, according to official statistics, now contributes 10 per cent towards the total gross domestic product (GDP). The most dynamic area within this market is that of modern residential and business centres that offer facilities and services for companies that rent or purchase such office premises. The demand for business premises in major cities (mainly in the capital, Tirana) is high and rising, and the construction industry is addressing this demand by building high quality and properly equipped buildings.

Notwithstanding this fact, the development of the real estate sector is hindered by uncertainty over ownership title, the long process of restitution and compensation of properties and the difficult process of registration of properties due to missing property documentation and unclear chain of title. Property disputes are among the most common cases heard in Albanian courts. This situation has also slowed down the expansion of foreign investment, particularly in tourism real estate, which is considered to be the key sector in the growth of the country.

Legal framework

The primary legislation that governs real estate law in Albania includes, *inter alia*:

- Albanian Civil Code (Law No. 7850 of 29 July 1994), as amended;
- Law on Land (No. 7501 of 19 July 1991), as amended;
- Law on Restitution and Compensation of Property (No. 9235 of 29 July 2004), as amended;
- Law on Sale and Purchase of Construction Land (No. 7980 of 27 July 1995);

- Law on Registration of Immovable Properties (No. 7843 of 13 July 1994), as amended;
- Law on Pastures and Meadows (No. 9693 of 19 March 2007);
- Law on Expropriation and Taking for Temporary Use of Private Properties for the Purposes of Public Interest (No. 8561 of 22 December 1999);
- Law on Urban Planning (No. 8405 of 17 September 1998), as amended; and
- Law on Tourism (No. 9734 of 14 May 2007), as amended.

Real estate registration

After the change of political system in 1991, private ownership of land was legally restored through the distribution of agricultural land to former collective farm members and farm employees in family ownership, the privatization of houses and the restitution of property to former owners.

In order to address this situation, and to register ownership of immovable properties and allow them to be made available for future transactions, a new system of registration of properties was introduced in 1994, entitled the Immovable Property Registration System (IPRS), otherwise known as the First Registration System.

The First Registration System consists of:

- assembling all documents from the archives;
- conducting a field survey;
- clarifying the physical definition of each plot of land and separately owned immovable object;
- accurate mapping; and
- cross-referencing of the archived documents that record ownership and subordinate rights with those documents held by physical and legal entities.

After the first registration process is completed, a unique certificate of title is issued, along with a plan of the property. The resulting information is reflected in the Kartela, which is a registry often consisting of volumes of pages, providing the legal position of the land on the date of first registration, including, but not limited to:

- the description of each property (size, boundaries and location); and
- title information (ownership, subordinate rights, encumbrances).

Subsequently, as transactions take place, changes are noted on the Kartela thus creating a chain of title. Failure to register a transaction shall render it null and void.

By referring to the Kartela at any time, an accurate and guaranteed certification can be produced in relation to the status of the property, its ownership, subsidiary rights and any encumbrances over the property.

The first registration process is yet to be completed throughout the entire territory of Albania, and its completion is hindered by a lack of clear ownership rights and claims for restitution or physical compensation by former owners. This is particularly true in areas of interest for tourism purposes. On the Albanian Riviera, comprising the most attractive areas of interest in this respect and situated in the south-west of the country, the first registration process is not yet complete.

Acquisition of real estate

After choosing a property to purchase, the first thing that must be done, prior to entering into any purchase agreement, is to check whether it is registered or not. If it is registered, the title and plan of the property must be verified at the Real Estate Registration Office. In the case of purchase of land, a comparison of the plan of the property with the actual layout and position of land is highly recommended.

After – and only after – verification of title, a sale-purchase agreement can be drafted (it is advisable to use a lawyer from a local firm for this), which must be executed as a notary deed before a notary public. Further to this, the agreement must be registered with the Real Estate Registration Office within 30 days of the date of execution of the contract; failure to so do will result in a penalty, which will be applied for every day of delay. After the registration of the conveyance agreement (ie. sale-purchase agreement) with the registry, a new certificate of title will be issued in favour of the purchaser.

It is often the case in Albania that property is purchased "off-plan", ie. it has not yet been built, therefore a certificate of title will not be passed to the purchaser until the property is built and sold with monies transferred. In this case, Albanian law permits a conditional sale-purchase contract, which is an oft-used agreement whereby the seller and purchaser specify amongst other matters the purchase price and method of payment, which is usually in instalments. Under the Albanian Civil Code, the ownership title cannot be transferred in such a conditional sale-purchase agreement until the final instalment has been made. This agreement should also be registered with the Real Estate Registration Office; however, it should be noted that until title is passed, the purchaser, in the event of any default, will not have any real rights in the property, but only personal, which means that he/she will only have a contractual claim for the loss of monies and possibly damages.

Only rights in a property that is registered can give rise to real property rights, ie. an ownership interest in the actual property. Non-registered rights give rise only to personal rights, which can only be redeemed through a claim for breach of contract, in which case the aggrieved party would usually only receive monetary compensation as opposed to any real rights in the property. This is why it is crucial to ensure that any property that is purchased is registered in the manner it is stated to be and that the stated owner actually is the registered owner.

There are, of course, property related taxes, which are not discussed in this analysis, for which prior advice should be sought when entering the real estate market in Albania.

Lease of immovable property

The period of lease of immovable properties may not be longer than 30 years, except as otherwise provided by specific law, eg. in various cases the state leases its territories for a period of 99 years under an emphyteusis contract. The period of a lease for dwellings may not be longer than five years. Any lease contract for a period of longer than one year should be in written form. Any lease agreement executed for a period longer than nine years should be registered with the Real Estate Registration Office. Furthermore, a lease contract for agricultural land longer than nine years should be executed before a notary public.

Foreign individuals or entities owning real estate in Albania may freely lease out their property, and, of course, the incomes generated will be subject to income tax.

Restitution issues

Prior to the end of Communism in 1991, all land and buildings fell under state ownership. After 1945, almost all land was nationalized, but it was the Constitution of 1976 that cemented the process of nationalization by abolishing the right of private ownership over land.

After 1991, Albania joined other East European countries in the transition towards a market economy, beginning with the privatization of state-owned properties. One element of the privatization process was the restitution and compensation of properties. In 1993, the first law governing the restitution of properties was enacted; it was abolished when a new law was introduced in 2004. The new law was amended in 2006.

The law of 1993 established the restitution of all unoccupied immovable properties located within the territory of a municipality, excluding agricultural land (which was distributed to former collective farm members and farm employees pursuant to the Law on Land (1991)) and compensation, both physical and financial.

The new law of 2004 extended the range of properties subject to restitution to include agricultural and non-agricultural land in areas of touristic interest as a priority. This amendment led to the submission of new claims. The amendments of 2006, *inter alia*, extended the deadline for submission of claims of former owners up to 1 October 2007, and there are suggestions that another extension should be provided for another one-year period, but such amendments have yet to be approved and published.

Foreign investment in real estate

According to Albanian foreign investment legislation, a foreign investor is:

- a foreign individual;
- a foreign legal entity incorporated under laws other than Albanian law; or
- a person who holds Albanian citizenship, permanently resides abroad and invests in Albania.

A foreign investment is any investment owned directly or indirectly by the foreign investor in:

- movables, immovable property, tangible or intangible property, as well as any other property right;
- a company whose rights from any kind of participation in a company— shares, loans, monetary obligations, etc.—are related to an investment; or
- any right recognized by law or contract and any licence or permission issued in pursuance with legislation in force.

Foreign investment in Albania is not subject to any preconditions. Foreign investors enjoy the same treatment as domestic investors in similar circumstances, except in the case of land ownership, which is governed by the special Law on the Sale of Construction Land and Law on the Conveyance of Title over Agricultural Land (1998).

In principle, a foreign investor may purchase buildings and the land on which such buildings are constructed without any restriction. According to the Law on the Sale of Construction Land, however, a foreign investor can buy vacant construction land only on condition that such land is used for construction and such construction is completed.

In order for the foreign investor to obtain title (giving rise to real rights over the land and property), the value of the investment completed (ie. the construction) must be at least three times that of the value of the land on which it is built. A special procedure is required to complete such transactions. The motive behind such a restriction is to compel foreigners to develop constructions and not merely use the land as a means of taking advantage of the increase in the market value of the land.

A foreigner is further prohibited from purchasing agricultural land. In order to circumvent this prohibition, in practice agricultural land is converted into land for construction through a special procedure for the approval of a project, and when the conversion is completed, the foreigner may enter into a deal with the owner in the same manner as in the case for construction land.

Despite the above restrictions, unconditional acquisition of land by foreigners, for either agricultural or construction purposes, is possible. A foreigner wishing to invest in such land can establish a company under Albanian law that is recognized as a domestic entity; however, this is a legally debatable solution and there is some risk attached to it, although it is often carried out in practice. The Albanian company will then be entitled to purchase land freely, although according to foreign investment law, an Albanian company established by a foreign investor is defined as a foreign investment itself, therefore any acquisition of land under such circumstances may be inferred as an investment owned indirectly by a foreign investor.

Expropriation and nationalization

The law on foreign investment provides that foreign investments will not be expropriated or nationalized directly or indirectly; they will not be the subject of any measure equal to these measures, except in special cases in the public interest, defined by law, without discrimination, and with immediate, appropriate and effective compensation, in accordance with legal procedures.

Real estate construction

Albania is still experiencing problems with urban planning. The biggest problem is that Albania still does not have approved urban plans even for its major cities. The current government, however, is making this issue a priority and efforts are being made to approve the master plan for the whole of the Albanian territory, in particular coastal areas. The lack of such master plans has led to a chaotic real estate development, particularly in the large cities where the investment interest in real estate has been very high.

According to the Law on Urban Planning, construction is only permitted upon the issue of a construction site permit and building permit granted by the relevant authorities, which are:

* the Local Planning Council for surface areas less than 5,000 square metres (sqm); and
* the National Planning Council for surfaces over 5,000 sqm.

Upon completion of the construction in compliance with the building permit, a permit to utilize the building will be issued by the local authorities. Upon the issue of this permit, the building may be registered with the Immovable Property Registration Office. There are many steps involved in acquiring the various permits/permissions required in order to pursue the construction of a building, which are not detailed here, and advice should be sought before proceeding with any construction.

Tourism-related investment

Since 1990, all elected governments have announced that tourism will be given top priority, citing Albania's potential for tourism, ie. geographical position, climate, important sites of archaeology and culture. These efforts were to some extent cemented in 1993, with the enactment of the Law on Priority Tourism Development Zones. However, the Law was reflective of the conditions and principal problems of that period.

The Law on Priority Tourism Development Zones introduced several incentives for those investing in relevant areas. These incentives applied to investors who had been granted the status of a "promoted person" by the ministry of tourism, culture, youth and sports. The main activities promoted were construction, reconstruction, improvement and extension, as well as operating processes for hotels, motels and resorts. The promoted person was entitled to enter into a lease agreement with the ministry of tourism, culture, youth and sports for an initial period of 25 years, with the right to renew the lease for a maximum of three consecutive 25-year periods, with the last period being 24 years, amounting to a 99-year lease. This law has now been abolished by the new law on tourism mentioned below, and any incentives that were provided therein no longer exist.

The relatively recent Law on Tourism consolidates the policies on the development of tourism in Albania (in addition to the special strategy on tourism of 2006) drafted in 2002 by the ministry of tourism, culture, youth and sports and adopted by the Council of Ministers in 2003. The principle of sustainable development of tourism is at the heart of this law and the key developments therein are:

- the willingness to regulate the field of tourism;
- the standardization of tourist services; and
- the attraction of foreign tourists, for which the law specifies certain minimum standards for the conditions of tourism.

In addressing other matters, this law provides that the standards, criteria and procedure for the establishment and recognition of a resort (constructed according to the status of "promoted person" granted under the previous law of 1993) shall be specified by a special regulation approved by order of the minister of tourism, culture, youth and sports, which is yet to be approved.

Contracts regarding tourist resorts entered into under the previous law of 1993 are now governed only by the Civil Code and, of course, the terms of the relevant contract. However, if such contracts are found not to be in compliance with the terms of the 1993 Law, the licensing standards and classification of the contract shall be unilaterally terminated.

2.15

Insurance Law

Kalo & Associates

Introduction

At present, insurance companies in Albania operate predominantly in the field of motor insurance, largely due to the fact that third party motor vehicle insurance is the only mandatory form of insurance. The insurance market has experienced rapid growth, and domestic companies have begun to expand their business operations outside Albania.

There are 10 large companies that are key players in the insurance market, most of which operate in the non-life insurance field. These companies are important in the promotion and growth of this market, much of which is due to the standards of auditing they use. According to recent surveys, all these companies are audited in accordance with International Financial Reporting Standards (IFRS).

The general opinion is that the primary legislation in this field is satisfactory, but that companies are not launching enough new products into the market, and further, those companies competing in the very few products currently available pay little attention to other forms of competition. Foreign companies are needed in this sector, as they can provide necessary cash injections as well as experience in order to further consolidate the market.

Although Albania is not yet part of the European Union (EU), it is party to a Stabilization and Association Agreement (SAA) with the EU that was signed on 12 June 2006. Pursuant to this important agreement, Albania and the EU shall cooperate in focusing on the key areas related to the insurance sector in its fulfilment of the *acquis communautaire*. The parties to this agreement shall further cooperate with the aim of establishing and developing a suitable framework for the promotion of the insurance sector. Thus any future changes in this field are likely to be reflective of EU standards and practices, as with other countries in the South East Europe (SEE) region that have either just entered or are seeking to enter the EU.

Legal framework

After the end of communist rule, Albania underwent great change and its legal framework had to be amended to support subsequent political and economic changes. Part of this change was the liberalization of the insurance sector and the establishment of private insurance.

The insurance market in Albania was governed by the Law on Insurance and Reinsurance Activities (No. 8081 of March 1996), as amended from time to time. The increasingly developing economic and business environment, however, required that a new law be enacted, and the Law on the Activity of Insurance, Reinsurance and Intermediation in Insurance and Reinsurance (No. 9267 of 29 July 2004) was approved.

The Albanian Civil Code (No. 7850 of 29 July 1994), as amended from time to time, also contains provisions for the contractual aspects of insurance relations and for contracts of personal insurance that may be entered into.

International treaties, conventions and charters also play an important role in insurance legislation in Albania, as they may be made compulsory through ratification by parliament.

Industry regulators

Financial Supervisory Authority

The Albanian Financial Supervisory Authority (FSA) is the regulatory body that is charged with the supervision and regulation of the insurance sector (ie. insurance service suppliers, business intermediaries and companies). It was established in 2006 as a means of consolidating the regulatory and supervisory functions of all financial services (except micro-lending activities, which remain under the regulation and jurisdiction of the Bank of Albania). The previously established Insurance Supervisory Authority and Securities Commission and Pension Funds Authority have now been disbanded, and their functions are carried out by the FSA.

The FSA is a central national institution that is independent of the government and reports to parliament on its activity on an annual basis. It is responsible for licensing, regulating and supervising the insurance, pension funds and securities sectors; it carries out its supervisory duties by off-site monitoring, on-site monitoring and setting up criteria for reporting.

Albanian Insurance Bureau

Insurance companies providing compulsory motor insurance must become members of the Albanian Insurance Bureau (AIB), also known as the Bureau. The AIB currently has eight members and is a legal entity. The statute governing the AIB is approved by the minister of finance.

The AIB's main powers are the administration of the Compensation Fund and of the Green Card Fund (the Green Card is required as proof that the minimum legal requirements in the EU for third party liability insurance in any country for which the Green Card is valid, amongst them Albania, are covered). In addition, the AIB has some other functions such as, inter alia:

- performing all duties in relation to its membership of the Council of Bureaus;
- representing its members in relations with international organizations in the field of motor insurance;
- ratifying agreements with similar organizations in other countries.

Association of Albanian Insurers

Membership of the Association of Albanian Insurers is voluntary. The mission of the association is:

(a) giving the insurance industry a public profile as a productive and progressive part of the structure of society;
(b) protecting its members' interests and supporting their insurance activities;
(c) harmonizing the efforts of all players on the insurance market;
(d) lobbying for the protection of the insurance industry in the process of drafting laws and amendments to law in favour of the insurance industry;
(e) introducing and supporting statements and proposals of its members when interacting with state authorities and international institutions;
(f) creating preconditions so as to avoid unfair competition.

Some five insurance companies are currently members of the association.

Setting up an insurance company

Insurance activities can only be carried out through an insurance company in Albania, which must be established as a joint-stock company in accordance with the Law on Commercial Companies (No. 7638 of 19 November 1992). When establishing an insurance or reinsurance company, a higher than the usual minimum of capital is required, ie at least 30 million Albanian leke (ALL) in cash.

Insurance business can only be carried out with the relevant licence, issued by the FSA. An application must be submitted to the FSA that contains:

- the name and legal seat;
- a list of the shareholders and information relating to them;

- information on the origination of the capital;
- a business plan;
- a list of the members of the managing body.

The FSA has the right to request further documents should it so deem appropriate. If the company fails to submit the required documentation, the FSA has the right to refuse to issue the licence.

The licence itself may be issued to an insurance company or branch of a foreign insurance company, to a reinsurance company or a branch of a foreign reinsurance company, and in all cases it is granted for an indefinite period. The licence cannot be assigned or transferred to third parties or sold to others. Duly licensed companies can perform insurance activities only within the category specified in the licence. The various types of licence provided for by law are:

- licence for the performance of the specifically requested insurance activity;
- licence for additional activities (for every new insurance class);
- licence for the performance of insurance activity by branches of foreign companies.

The licence may be withdrawn in the following events:

- the company does not begin its activity within six months of the issue of the licence;
- the company suspends activity for more than six months;
- the company initiates a bankruptcy procedure;
- the company initiates a liquidation procedure;
- the insurance contract is transferred to another company;
- the submitted documents were falsified or untrue.

The FSA will notify the applicant of its preliminary refusal or approval and in the latter case, the applicant can then register with the Tirana Court of First Instance as an insurance company. Upon presentation to the FSA of the court registration and various other related documents, the company will be issued with its licence. The decision-making process should take two months. Note that from September 2007, company registration takes place at the National Registration Centre.

Classes of insurance

The law recognizes various different classes and types of insurance cover, and though many are not utilized, they are nevertheless available in law. There are some 23 classes of insurance cover classified within the following categories:

- accident and health insurance;
- motor vehicle insurance;
- marine and transport insurance;
- aircraft insurance;
- fire and other property damage insurance;
- liability insurance;
- credit and guarantee insurance;
- life insurance.

The law defines insurance as "…the transfer of an eventual risk, financial loss or material damage from the insured to the insurer in accordance with an insurance contract".

Some of the more common types of insurance that fall into the above categories are as follows:

1. insurance for accidents (including industrial injury and disease). This covers the immediate payment of the total sum (or instalments) agreed for the compensation of damage and payment due to injury, health abnormalities or death;
2. insurance for disease, which covers a fixed financial income for incapacity resulting from health issues, and/or remuneration of hospital expenses;
3. insurance for land motor vehicles, rolling stock, airplanes and ships (damage and loss);
4. insurance of civil liability arising out of the use of vehicles mentioned in (3) above (including carrier's liability);
5. insurance for civil liabilities not mentioned above;
6. insurance for goods during transport (including goods, luggage, and all other items) and for all damage to or loss of goods during transport and damage to or loss of luggage, regardless of the method of transport;
7. insurance for fire and natural catastrophes, including explosion, storm, nuclear accident or landslide;
8. insurance for credit;
9. insurance for guarantee;
10. insurance for cover of different financial losses, including those incurred as a result of employment risk, insufficient income, loss of market value and indirect loss due to trading, unforeseen commercial expenditure, etc.;
11. insurance for legal protection (including cover of legal and judicial expenses);
12. life insurance (including, *inter alia*, life-death insurance and life insurance connected to investment funds).

Companies that choose to provide and be active in the field of non-life insurance cannot perform life-insurance business and vice versa, although a reinsurance company can perform both life and non-life insurance business. Companies seeking to conduct business in the insurance industry shall usually only be licensed to provide insurance services in the classes that it specifically requests.

Insurance contracts

The Albanian Civil Code defines the insurance contract and the obligations thereof. It provides that an insurance contract must be agreed in writing, by an insurance policy that the insurer issues to the insured in order for it to be valid. The policy should include, amongst other details:

(a) the name of the insurer;
(b) the name of the insured in the case of personal insurance;
(c) the location of the property in the case of property insurance;
(d) the insured event;
(e) the duration of the contract; and
(f) the value (if applicable), the amount and terms of payment of the premium.

The provisions of the Code assume that the contract is dissolved if the insured risk ceases after agreement of the contract, but this does not apply to obligatory insurance or maritime insurance, which are regulated by separate provisions. Thus the insured party is required to notify the insurer of any change in circumstances; this is also necessary for any amendment to the amount of the insurance premium.

The Code also specifies the loss of the right to payment if the insured party does not notify the insurer of the verified occurrence of an event within the period of time specified in the contract.

Limitations and specific circumstances

Below is a non-exhaustive list of terms which the Civil Code stipulates if not otherwise specified in the contract:

1. The limitation of liability compensation in the event of death, loss of work capacity, and damage to property incurred as a result of acts of war is specified.
2. Property insurance compensates the loss of profit only if it is expressly provided for in the contract.
3. The beneficiary of an insurance contract may be a third party, who has the right to accept the terms of the contract entered into even after verification of the insured event.
4. With regard to personal insurance, in the event of the death of the insured party, the amount paid to the beneficiary is not included in the inheritable assets of the insured. Furthermore, the payment is due regardless of any sums that may be paid by social security.

2.16

Environmental Law

Kalo & Associates

Introduction

The legal framework relating to the environment in Albania is comprehensive and in compliance with international conventions agreed to or ratified by the Albanian government. However, the level of implementation of the law is not optimal and the state does not properly exercise its authority to fully implement the laws on protection of the environment.

Environmental history

In Albania, as in the other East European countries, the beginning of the 1990s marked a deep change in the economic and political system, due to the introduction of capitalism. Factors which have had a negative impact on Albanian society with respect to the environment can be divided into pre-1990 and post-1990 factors.

Pre-1990 factors

Prior to 1990, the environmental factors were as follows:

* the disorderly cutting of trees;
* land erosion;
* air pollution caused by industrial plants and factories; and
* inappropriate management and treatment of industrial and urban waste, the impact of which was mainly noticed in the ecosystems of rivers and lakes.

Post-1990 factors

After 1990, the failure and impotence of the relevant government bodies to protect the environment had far-reaching effects. In addition, during the early years of the 1990s, the lack of state authority, economic difficulties, as well as the lack of government strategy and policy for demographic migration, had a critical impact on the environment. These effects are outlined below.

Flora and fauna

There was widespread destruction of forests and plant life, and fauna and flora were irreversibly damaged. Aggressive hunting through massive eradication destroyed river and sea fauna and even with the introduction of new laws and measures such phenomena are still occurring. Various rare species of fowl are extinct or have migrated to other regions.

Health hazards

Urban pollution and the failure of proper treatment and management of such waste is a serious health risk. The uncontrolled development of the construction and real estate sectors, the high level of corruption and the greed for profits have created solid waste and residues which are extremely hazardous for citizens living in big cities.

Pollution

Air pollution levels in big cities as Tirana, Elbasan, etc. are much higher than the permitted level. During the last five years, pollution from vehicles, construction, or toxic materials produced by the burning of the waste and garbage have consistently worsened air quality.

There is a lack of education and information amongst the public regarding the environment. To be concerned about the environment in Albania is still considered a luxury, considering the economic problems that the majority of the Albanian population is facing (lack of water, electricity, etc). Sanitary conditions in the cities show the low level of awareness in the community and the lack of serious involvement of state bodies in resolving such problems.

Legal framework

Pre-1990

Before the end of socialism in Albania, legislation relating to the environment was relatively poor. Legislation contained general provisions and protection of the environment was not a priority for the government of that period. The legal framework did not strictly regulate the protection of the environment despite the investment and the operation of plants in the steel, iron, coal, oil and chemical industries. During this period, such activity became a hazardous source of environmental pollution and legislation did not provide for the requirement of environmental licences or other administrative measures. Sanctions were inconsiderable and institutional organizations were not efficient in monitoring such problems.

Environmental protection was considered an ancillary issue that was of no importance while the priority of the government was production and the achievement of goals, with no consideration for their consequences and impact on the environment. Since the Albanian economy was a state economy, the biggest polluter of the environment was the state. All these factors contributed to the deterioration of various ecosystems which cannot be restored or adjusted without considerable investment and long-term plans.

Post-1990

After 1990, the environment was considered, at least formally, an important issue and in the public interest. The first laws on the protection of the environment were approved in the early 1990s, filling the legal gap in that field.

However, after the new Albanian Constitution entered into force in 1998, a whole new legal framework was adopted. The Albanian Constitution provides that the state aims to create a healthy and ecologically appropriate environment for present and future generations, and rational exploitation of the forests, waters, meadows and other natural resources.

Legislation

The key applicable legislation in this sector includes the following:

- Law on Protection of the Environment (2002);
- Law on Environmental Impact Assessment (2003);
- Law on Protected Areas (2003);
- Law on Protection of Air from Pollution (2002);
- Law on Protection of Marine Environment from Pollution and Damage (2002);
- Law on Protection of Transboundary Lakes (2003);
- Law on Chemical Substances and Materials (2003);
- Law on Environmental Treatment of Polluted Waters (2003);
- Law on Environmental Treatment of Solid Waste (2003);
- Law on the Protection of Vegetation (2005);
- Law on the Forests and Forestry Service (2005);
- Law on Protection of Environment from Cross-border Impacts (2007);
- Law on Evaluation and Management of Noise in the Environment (2007);
- Law on Treatment of Hazardous Waste (2006); and

- Law on the Designation of Rules and Procedures for the International Treatment of Endangered Species of Fauna and Wild Flora (2008).

Environmental protection law

Protecting the environment against pollution and damage constitutes a national priority for all state institutions, physical and legal entities, and foreigners and nationals who operate their enterprises within Albanian territory.

The purpose of the 2002 law is to regulate relations between humans and the environment, protect aspects of the environment, and process and guarantee the conditions for sustainable development by establishing the necessary legal framework for the implementation of the constitutional right to have an ecologically sound environment. The law aims to achieve:

- the rational use of the environment, including:
  - the reduction of discharges into and pollution of the environment;
  - damage prevention; and
  - the rehabilitation and restoration of damaged environment;
- the improvement of environmental conditions related to the quality of life and protection of public health;
- the preservation and maintenance of natural resources, renewable and non-renewable, and a rational and efficient system of ensuring their regeneration;
- the coordination of state activities to meet the requirements of environmental protection;
- international cooperation in the field of environmental protection;
- the promotion of public participation in environmental protection activities;
- the coordination of economic and social development of the country with the requirements of environmental protection and sustainable development; and
- the establishment and strengthening of the institutional system of environmental protection on a national and local level.

Under this law, the basic elements of environmental protection are:

- the prevention and reduction of pollution of water, air, soil and pollution of any kind;
- the conservation of biological diversity according to the country's natural and bio-geographical background;
- the rational use of natural and mineral resources and the avoidance of their over-exploitation;

- the ecological restoration of areas damaged by human activity or other natural destructive phenomena; and
- the preservation of ecological balance and life quality improvement.

The government's environmental policies and strategies include the national strategy on the environment, sector strategies, laws governing specific sectors, and national and local action plans.

Activity which may have a significant impact on the environment is required to undergo an Environmental Impact Assessment before approval and implementation of the project.

Policies, plans and programmes on the development of transport, energy, tourism, industry, services, territory adjustment, and economic and social development in general are subject to a Strategic Environmental Assessment.

All relevant parties must take part in the Environment Impact Assessment and Strategic Environment Assessment process, especially local government bodies and public and environmental not-for-profit organizations.

Environmental permits

For activity that will have an environmental impact, interested parties must obtain approval from the relevant authority. Approval of the request to carry out such activity is granted by issuing an environmental declaration, environmental permit, consent or authorization. Environmental declarations are awarded by the minister of the environment and provide the technical and legal reasoning behind them, and include the relevant actions and measures to be taken in order to avoid or reduce any negative impact on the environment.

The exploitation of minerals and natural resources, the operation of installations for their utilization and technological processing and other activities which have an impact on the environment and require an environmental permit are defined by decisions of the Council of Ministers. The minister of the environment has the requisite power and authority to issue, reject, review or amend an environmental permit.

The process of issuing an environmental permit is open and transparent to all concerned parties, including, in the case of any trans-boundary impact on the environment, other states. Activities that affect the environment cannot be undertaken without the existence of an environmental permit. Activities having an impact on the environment which take place without a permit shall be suspended, closed down, or partially or completely stopped by the Environmental Inspectorate. Physical and legal entities shall carry out, at their own expense, an environmental assessment of the activities they undertake no less then once every three years. Furthermore, the environmental assessment must adhere to the methodology approved by the minister of the environment.

Environmental monitoring

Environmental monitoring is obligatory. The ministry of the environment, in cooperation with other central and local bodies, is responsible for the National Monitoring Programme, and also coordinates and controls the work for its implementation. The ministry of the environment controls the quality of monitoring, the measures taken, the application of methodologies and qualification of participating specialists, and the equipment used, as well as the reliability of results. The ministry of the environment prepares the National Register on discharges, releases and transfers of pollutants into the environment, and the use of water, energy, mineral and natural resources.

The Environmental Inspectorate and Regional Environmental Agencies supervise the state of the environment. Such control is permanently exercised, continuously and repeatedly, in accordance with the parameters, sources and causes of environmental pollution or damage. Forest Police, Construction Police, the Sanitary Inspectorate, the Plant Protection Inspectorate, the Fishery Inspectorate, the Hydrocarbons Inspectorate, the Zoo-Veterinary Inspectorate and the controlling bodies of local governments, according to their relevant jurisdiction, exercise controls on the basis of the normative acts that regulate the specific activities of these bodies.

The Environmental Inspectorate has the authority to decide, on a case-by-case basis, to close down, suspend, partially or completely, or stop the activity of physical and legal entities that have caused environmental pollution or damage, and stipulate the relevant tasks for the improvement of the situation.

The law provides that in the case of any threats or damage to, or pollution of the environment, citizens, the public and not-for-profit organizations have the right to ask the relevant state bodies to take appropriate measures within set deadlines and in accordance with their authority provided for by the law, or they may file a lawsuit with the court against the public body or physical or legal entity that has damaged the environment or is likely to damage it.

Violations and penalties

When the violations of this law constitute a criminal act, the Environmental Inspectorate can file an application to initiate criminal proceedings. The law provides that violations which are not criminal actions are considered administrative violations and are subject to sanctions with fines starting from 10,000 Albanian leke (ALL) up to ALL 1 million. Aside from the penalties, the sequestration of the means and substances that pollute or damage the environment is also decided upon. In addition, depending upon the level of pollution or damage already caused, the permit may be temporarily or permanently withdrawn. The State Police may become involved in the case of obstruction or opposition to the application of the above-mentioned measures.

The decision to set a fine is open to formal appeal which can be submitted within 10 days of the notification of the decision to set a fine. The minister must decide on the issue within 15 days from the filing of the appeal. The decision of the minister is subject to further appeal before Tirana District Court. The income collected from the fines is deposited with the state budget within 30 days of the date of the final decision. For every day of delay after this deadline, up to a further deadline of 30 days, the person at fault must pay, in addition to the penalty, a sum equal to 10 per cent of the penalty. The Chief Inspector or the minister of the environment can order the suspension or the permanent closure of the activity of subjects that do not comply with the legal deadlines, measures and sanctions determined by the Environmental Inspectorate. This measure may also be taken against an entity in the event that it commits that same offence again within a calendar year. Suspension or permanent closure is undertaken according to the level of danger that the activity represents to health and the environment. The decision on suspension or closure of activity by the Chief Inspector or the minister of the environment can be appealed to the district court within five days of the date of receipt of the notification of the decision.

Environmental impact assessment law

This law aims to set up a regulatory framework for the general, integrated and timely assessment of the environmental impact of proposed projects or activities, thus preventing or reducing negative impacts on the environment. Further, it aims to establish an open assessment process, impartially administered through the participation of central and local bodies, the public and environmental not-for-profit organizations, of project proposals and physical and legal entities specializing in this field.

This law sets forth rules, procedures, deadlines, rights and duties in the following areas:

- the identification and assessment of the direct and indirect impact of projects or activities in the area of the environment in which they will be implemented;
- an assessment of the impact of proposed projects and how it would compare if certain variations were made to the following areas:
  - place;
  - measure and capacity; and
  - technology.

A comparison will also be made with the state of the environment if the project is not implemented and an assessment of measures to prevent and minimize damage to the environment will be undertaken.

Anyone who intends to carry out projects which will have an impact on the environment is subject to an "advanced", or full, environmental impact assessment or a "summary", or less detailed, environmental impact assessment. Furthermore, strategies and action plans on energy, mines, industry, transport, agriculture, forests, natural resources and management of mining properties, waste management, as well as territorial adjustment, national and regional plans of urban and rural centres, industrial areas, coastal areas, areas of tourism, protected areas and highly polluted areas sensitive to damage are subject to a Strategic Environmental Assessment.

The request for approval of the project is filed with the Regional Environmental Agency.

Environmental impact assessment reports are the primary documents upon which the approval of project is based. Such reports are prepared by licensed physical and legal entities. After reviewing the data presented in the report, the Regional Environmental Agency shall consult with local government agencies and prepare in writing its own justified opinion in approving or denying the project and it shall forward its opinion to the minister of the environment.

The minister of the environment will require an opinion as to whether the project conforms to national and regional development programmes and plans, and the expected level of impact on the environment; therefore he/she will forward the description of the project and the full environmental impact assessment report to:

- central bodies responsible for the area covered by the proposed project;
- urban and tourism development organizations;
- local government bodies in the geographic area in which the project will be implemented; and
- institutions specializing in environmental impact assessment.

The project description and report on the environmental impact assessment shall undergo a public debate with the participation of interested parties. Interested public and environmental not-for-profit organizations will participate in all phases of the impact assessment decision-making process.

Violations and penalties

Seeking approval of a project founded on false declarations, falsified documents or information constitutes an administrative offence, punishable by a fine of ALL 50,000–300,000 according to the degree of the contravention. The fine will be imposed and executed by the Environmental Inspectorate.

The imposition of a fine is open to formal appeal before the minister of the environment within 10 days; in the event that minister does not respond within 15 days, an appeal can be made before the court. When these violations constitute a criminal offence, the ministry of the environment may initiate a request for criminal prosecution.

Law of protected areas

The object of this law is the preservation, administration, management and usage of protected areas and their natural and biological resources. The purpose is to provide special protection for important components of natural reserves, biodiversity and nature as a whole, through the establishment of protected areas. Protected areas are set to provide the preservation and regeneration of natural habitats, species, natural reserves and landscapes.

Protected areas are considered land, water, sea and coastal territories designated as such for the protection of biodiversity, cultural and natural characteristics. The law provides in detail the categories of protected areas, in addition to providing the definition and criteria of what shall be considered to be the following:

* a natural reserve;
* a national park;
* a natural monument;
* a managed natural reservation;
* a protected landscape;
* a protected area of managed resources;
* forests;
* waters; and
* other natural characteristics within protected areas.

The declaration of a protected area and the surrounding buffer zone will be decided by the Council of Ministers, upon the recommendation of the minister of the environment, and that is after the submission of the opinion of local government units, specialized institutions, non-governmental organizations (NGOs) and private owners, if such are included in their properties. The ministry of the environment, other state bodies and local governments will prepare management plans for each protected area, sometimes in collaboration with third parties. All management plans for protected areas which are not prepared by the ministry of the environment will be endorsed by this ministry in order to ensure conformity with the objectives of this law or of other related laws.

Given that Albania faces many problems with regard to the process of restitution of property to ex-owners, it may be a problem if the protected area is within a privately-owned property. In such cases, the law provides that the owners and users of land that is to be declared to be a protected area, as well as any individual or authority having an interest in the area, shall have the right to object before the ministry of the environment. The ministry of the environment shall review objections within one month and shall notify the interested parties of the decision taken. The decision of the ministry is open to appeal before the relevant district court within 15 days of the notification. Private owners are not permitted to intervene or damage protected areas within their property; however, territories and private objects included in protected areas will remain private property. They will be administered and used by the owner or by the legal user only according to the requirements of the management plan of the area, endorsed by the ministry of the environment.

Violations and penalties

The ministry of the environment is responsible for monitoring the protected areas, in cooperation with public or private institutions. A protected area can lose its status or have it changed, according to this law, when circumstances and the objectives behind the reason for the giving of such status have changed. This shall be decided by the Council of Ministers upon the collection of opinions from specialist institutions, local government bodies, not-for-profit organizations and from owners, where their estates are part of a protected area. The removal of the protected status shall also apply to the buffer zone.

Violations of the provisions of this law, which do not constitute a criminal offence, shall constitute administrative infringement.

Air pollution protection law

The purpose of this law is to guarantee the right of citizens to clean air, and to protect human health, fauna, flora and the natural and cultural values of the Albanian environment from air pollution. The norms of air quality, deposit norms and norms for specific parts of the country are approved by the Council of Ministers upon the recommendation of the ministry of the environment and ministry of health.

Air pollution is restricted by the establishment and enforcement of discharge norms, established on the basis of EU norms. The Council of Ministers establishes the permitted level of discharge based upon recommendations from the ministry of the environment.

In the case of sources of industrial pollution which existed before the introduction of this law and which are unable to comply with the new legal standards due to technological constraints (ie. they are not sufficiently technologically developed), the minister of the environment can define provisional norms. These provisional norms and the manner of their establishment must nevertheless be approved by the Council of Ministers. Norms of discharge from mobile sources are approved by a joint decision of the ministry of the environment and ministry of transport and telecommunications.

Every person is obliged to preserve the cleanliness of the air, to protect it from pollution that may arise from activities they carry out in the territory of Albania. This law prohibits the use of fuels, other than those defined by the manufacturer of the relevant equipment, as prescribed in the accompanying operating instructions. This law requires the use of only the best possible modern technology in the construction of new works and in the renovation of existing ones.

The Council of Ministers, upon the recommendation of the minister of the environment and minister of health, designates those parts of the country having high levels of pollution as areas requiring special air protection. For such specially-protected areas, the minister of the environment, minister of health and local government units design special measures for the protection of air quality. In these specially-protected areas, for the purposes of regulation, special smog detection and signalling systems are established, and emergency measures are defined to be applied by government bodies and operators to bring the situation under control. Upon the recommendation of the ministry of the environment, the Council of Ministers approves the criteria for the establishment and operation of smog detection systems.

Every operator discharging pollutants into the air must provide detailed information to the public air pollution data and to periodically provide to the ministry of the environment.

Any person who intends to operate facilities which may pollute the air must obtain joint permits from the ministry of the environment and local government. Operators polluting the air are obliged to pay discharge taxes based on the amount and type of discharged pollutants.

Violations and penalties

For the purposes of this law, when violations do not qualify as criminal offences and therefore amount to administrative infringements, the offenders are liable for fines ranging from ALL 10,000 to ALL 1 million. The Environmental Inspectorate is the authority that administers and executes fines and the suspension or termination of activity in accordance with this legislation.

In cases when such violations constitute criminal offences, the Environmental Inspectorate will impose charges against the polluting source.

Part Three

Finance Issues

3.1

Direct Corporate Taxation

Deloitte, Albania

In Albania, taxes are levied by the ministry of finance in cooperation with the Albanian government, and also by local government bodies.

Income is taxed in Albania in accordance with the provisions of the Income Tax Law (No. 8438, dated 28 December 1998). The ministry of finance (Department of Revenue) through the General Taxation Department (GTD)—tax authority—implements and administers direct tax laws.

Taxable entities and residency

Albania follows a residence-based taxation system. Broadly, taxpayers may be classified as "residents" or "non-residents". A resident company is a company formed and registered under the Law on Commercial Companies (No. 9901, dated 14 April 2008) or one whose control and management is situated wholly in Albania. The fiscal year in Albania runs from 1 January to 31 December of each calendar year for all taxpayers. Taxable profit will be determined for the taxable period on the basis of the income statement, balance sheet and its annexes, which must be prepared in accordance with the Law on Accounting and Financial Statements (No. 9228, dated 29 April 2004), as well as relevant rules and regulations issued by the ministry of finance.

Resident taxpayers are subject to corporate income tax for taxable profit derived from all sources, within or outside the territory of the Republic of Albania. Non-resident taxpayers are subject to corporate income tax for all income derived from sources within the Republic of Albania.

Corporate income tax shall be imposed on:

- legal entities established according to the Law on Commercial Companies and registered for value-added tax (VAT) purposes;
- legal entities established in accordance with the Civil Code and which conduct profitable business in the territory of the Republic of Albania;
- other legal entities established or recognized as such per specific laws;
- partnerships;

- legal entities, partnerships or other groups of persons established or organized under a foreign law and conducting business activities through a Permanent Establishment on the territory of the Republic of Albania; and
- any other person, regardless of the legal form of registration, including physical persons, who are not subject to simplified profit tax, but are registered for VAT purposes.

Exemptions

All the entities below are exempted from corporate income tax:

- central and local government bodies;
- the Bank of Albania;
- legal entities which conduct only religious, humanitarian, educational activity;
- trade unions or chambers of commerce;
- foundations or non-bank financial institutions that are aimed at supporting developing policies of the government through credit granting;
- houses for producing cinematograph films;
- international organizations, agencies of technical cooperation and their representatives of which the exemption from taxes is established by specific agreements; and
- persons provided for in international agreements, which have been ratified by parliament.

Tax compliance

Generally, taxpayers are liable to make corporate income tax payments as advance payments by no later than the 15th of each month, and the method of calculation of each prepayment is defined by the Income Tax Law.

According to the Income Tax Law and Instruction No. 5, dated 18 January 2006, a new company will need to make an assessment of their future estimated corporate income tax and make a prepayment no later than the 15th of each month. However, a company involved in production activities would not need to prepay any corporate income tax on its first six months of operations.

All established companies must submit an annual declaration no later than 31 March of the subsequent year. Monthly prepayment is calculated depending on the last two years' corporate income tax, by separate calculation for the first four months, January–April, and the rest of the year, May–December.

Tax base

Generally, expenses incurred for business purposes are deductible from taxable income. The requirement for deductibility of expenses is that the expenses must be wholly and exclusively incurred for business purposes, and this must be supported by relevant documentation.

Depreciation on specified capital assets at prescribed rates is also deductible.

Expenditures not recognized for tax purposes

To determine the corporate income tax for a taxable period, it is important to recognize expenses which are not deductible (non-deductible expenses), as follows:

- the cost of land and building site acquisition and reclaiming;
- the cost of acquisition, improvement, renovation, and reconstruction of assets of businesses which are depreciated according to Article 22 of the Income Tax Law;
- an increase of basic capital of the company or contribution of each person in a partnership;
- costs of profit in kind;
- voluntary pension contributions;
- dividends declared and profit shared among partners or shareholders of commercial companies, as well as profit in the case of a partnership;
- interest paid which extend the 12-month average rate of the bank market, as officially published by the Bank of Albania;
- fines, late interest payments and other penal sanctions;
- creation or increase of reserves and other special funds except when it is defined otherwise by the Income Tax Law or specific rules;
- personal income tax, excise duties, corporate income tax and VAT;
- representation expenses and expenses for reception that exceed of 0.3 per cent of the entity's annual turnover;
- personal living and family expenses as defined by the minister of finance;
- expenses which exceed limits established by law or specific rules. The current limits are 3 per cent and 5 per cent of profit before corporate income tax for different sponsorship and for sponsorships of publishing houses, respectively;
- expenses for gifts;
- any expense which the taxpayer does not certify through a document;
- expenses for technical services, consultancy and management invoiced by third persons but not paid by the taxpayer within the tax period;
- losses, damages, scraps during production, transiting or warehouse;
- exceeding norms defined by legal and sub-legal act;

- salaries, bonuses and any other form of personal income, which are not paid to employees through the banking system;
- expenses of construction work which are invoiced from physical persons to construction companies;
- interest paid on loans and prepayments shall not be deductible to the extent that the loan or prepayment for which the interest is paid exceeds, on average, four times the amount of equity (own capital stock) during the taxable period. This restriction is not applicable to banks, insurance companies and leasing companies.

Inventory valuation

At the end of the taxable period, inventory is assessed using one of the defined methods in the Law on Accounting and Financial Statements; thus it is required to be systematically applied.

Depreciation

In order to define taxable profit, the taxpayer calculates the depreciation of the assets of the company according to prescribed rates, which vary depending upon the underlying asset category, as follows:

- Land, building sites, fine art, antiquaries, jewels, precious metals and stones are not depreciable.
- Costs of purchase or construction and costs of improvement, restoration, and reconstruction of buildings, machinery and equipment which serve for the long term will be calculated on a linear basis at the rate of 5 per cent per year, for a period of 20 years.
- Costs of purchase of intangible assets will be calculated on a linear basis at the rate of 15 per cent per year.
- Depreciation for the two following categories of assets will be calculated on the basis of a pooling system, with the following percentages applicable:
  - computers, information systems, software products, and equipment for database back-up at 25 per cent; and
  - all other assets of business activity at a rate of 20 per cent per year.

Reserves and provisions

After having paid corporate income tax, commercial companies are required to have their financial results of the previous year approved by either the shareholders' meeting or other decision-making body of the company. In addition, the shareholders' meeting or other decision-making body of the company must determine how the profit will be used after tax, for instance by defining a legal reserve amount, an amount to be used for investment purposes or for capital increase, or an amount to be distributed in the form of dividends.

Introduction of IFRS (NAS/IAS)

Starting from 1 January 2008, in accordance with the 2004 Accounting Law and the Instruction on National Accounting Standards (No. 4292, dated 15 June 2006), 14 International Standards became applicable to all private and public sector entities that have juridical status as "for profit" or "covering the costs".

Starting from 1 January 2008, the National Accounting Standards (NAS) are no longer applicable to those entities which use International Accounting Standards (IAS) and International Financial Reporting Standards (IFRS), such as banks, insurance companies, public entities that are financed by budgetary funds, and other private entities which would be designated by a decision of the ministry of finance. IFRS reporting became mandatory as of 1 January 2008, as specified by the published Order on Mandatory International Financial Reporting Standards and Financial Statements and Translated in Albanian (No. 65, dated 5 May 2008).

Tax rates

Corporate income tax

Annual corporate income tax is levied on income earned for the financial year as per the rates declared by the annual Finance Act.

As noted above, a resident company is generally subject to tax on its worldwide income. Effective 1 January 2008, the corporate income tax rate was reduced to 10 per cent.

Dividends

Dividends and distributions of earnings shall not be excluded in determining taxable profit of a resident person.

However, domestic dividends and distributions of earnings are exempt from the corporate income tax of the resident recipient company, when such dividends are distributed from companies that are subject to corporate income tax, and when the beneficiary resident's shareholding comprises at least 25 per cent of the value or of voting rights.

No participation exemption is in place for holdings of foreign companies. Consequently, dividends received from foreign companies will be included in taxable income.

Capital gains, losses and wealth tax

Capital gains on the sale of a company's fixed assets are taxed as part of the company's business income. There is no special tax rate applicable to capital gains.

Tax incentives

The government might decide occasionally to exempt an entity from corporate income tax for a period as determined by parliament, according to the Law on Participation of the Private Sector on Public Services and Infrastructure.

Special tax regimes are provided under the following laws:

* the Law on Development Zones of Tourism Industry (No. 7665, dated 21 January 1993);
* the Law on the Status of the Blind People (No. 8098, dated 28 March 1996); and
* the Decree on the Fiscal System on Hydrocarbons (No. 782, dated 22 February 1994).

Tax credits

If a resident generates profits or income from sources outside the Republic of Albania during a taxable period, the tax payable on that profit or income by that resident will be reduced by the amount of the tax payable with respect to those profits or income. The amount of foreign tax payable must be substantially certified by an authentic document as defined by the ministry of finance.

However, a reduction in personal income tax or corporate income tax cannot exceed the tax payable on profit or income generated from a foreign source if such income was generated in the Republic of Albania.

Carry forward of losses

If taxable profit results in losses in a taxable period, these losses may be offset by the profits generated in the following three taxable periods. This is applied according to principle "the first loss before the last one". Carry-backs of tax losses to previous taxable years are not permitted.

If during that taxable year, more than 25 per cent of direct or indirect ownership of the capital or voting rights of the company is transferred, pre-existing losses may no longer be carried forward.

Group tax treatment

Consolidation

No provisions currently exist for the grouping/consolidation of losses of entities within the same group.

Inter-company dividends

According to Article 26 and Article 33 of Income Tax Law, dividend proceeds are excluded from withholding tax when distributed from resident companies that are subject to corporate income tax and the beneficiary subject owns at least 25 per cent, in value or number, of the stock capital or voting rights.

Thin capitalization

The tax deduction for interest paid on loans (from shareholders and associated parties) is restricted where:

- the debt to equity ratio is 4:1 or above. Banks, insurance and leasing companies are not subject to this rule; and
- on interest paid which exceeds the 12-month average rate of the bank market, as officially published by the Bank of Albania.

Transfer pricing

Albania has not published its own transfer pricing guidelines. In practice, the Albanian tax authorities regularly refer to the Organization for Economic Cooperation and Development for guidance in applying transfer pricing principles. This practice is established by Article 36 of the Income Tax Law, and Instruction No. 5, dated 18 January 2006.

If the conditions of commercial and financial relationships between interacting entities are different from those of non-related entities, the tax authorities may decide that the taxable profit of any of these entities should include the profit it could have arrived at if such conditions did not exist. To properly and effectively apply Article 36 of the Income Tax Law, the tax administration may enter into an avoidance agreement with persons who carry on businesses with related entities, ensuring that their specific conditions do not change from those that may exist among non-related persons.

Taxation of non-residents

A non-resident company is generally subject to tax on income from Albanian sources.

Withholding taxes

All legal entities, partnerships, physical persons, Albanian resident traders, central and local government authorities and non-profit organizations are required to withhold tax at the rate of 10 per cent from the gross payments sourced within the territory of the Republic of Albania. However, a reduced withholding tax rate may apply under the application of a double taxation treaty.

Withholding tax is applied to the payment of dividends, interest, profit remittance and distribution, copyrights and royalties and technical, management, financial and insurance services. It is also applied to payments to management and board members, consulting services, payments for construction, installations, assembly or respective supervisory work, rental payments and payments for the performance of actors, musicians or sportspersons.

International transport is not subject to withholding tax.

Table 1. Withholding tax rates

Payments to:	Interest	Dividends	Royalties	Other income
Resident companies/ individuals that are not subject to corporate income tax or simplified profit tax	10%	10%	10%	10%
Non-resident companies/ individuals	10%	10%	10%	10%

Double taxation treaties

Double taxation hampers movement of individuals, companies, capital and reciprocal investments from one country to another. Bilateral tax agreements on the elimination of double taxation, through provisions designed and negotiated by contracting parties eliminate double taxation by defining the taxing right of each party on certain income of the entity, or by proportioning this right to tax between the contracting states, thus avoiding double taxation of the entity.

For countries that have Double Tax Avoidance Agreements with Albania, bilateral relief is available to a resident in respect of foreign taxes paid.

Albania has signed tax treaties with numerous countries. Treaties are currently in force with the following countries: Belgium, Bulgaria, Croatia, Czech Republic, Egypt, France, Greece, Hungary, Italy, FYR Macedonia, Malaysia, Malta, Moldova, Montenegro, the Netherlands, Norway, Poland, China, Romania, Russia, Serbia, Sweden, Switzerland, Turkey, Austria (effective on 1 January 2009) and Kosovo (UNMIK). Albania has signed tax treaties with other countries which are not yet in force: Korea (Rep), Latvia and Slovenia.

3.2

Indirect Corporate Taxation

Deloitte, Albania

Indirect taxes

Legal and regulatory environment

Tax related laws are drafted by the ministry of finance and approved by the parliament. The ministry of finance implements and administers indirect tax laws through the General Directorate of Taxes and General Directorate of Customs. Guidance and clarifications are issued by the General Directorate of Taxes in particular to supplement indirect tax laws related to value-added tax (VAT). Issues involving the interpretation of tax laws are decided by the judiciary, which is independent of the legislature.

Types of indirect taxes

Customs duties

Customs duties are levied on the import of goods into Albania at the rates specified in the Customs Tariff Law (No. 7609, dated 22 September 1992). Customs duties are prescribed based on customs tariffs, which are detailed in the annex to the above-mentioned law.

There are three categories of customs duties used in Albania:

1. tax on the value: calculated as a percentage of the value of goods that will be taxed;
2. specific duty: calculated as a fixed amount per item of the goods that will be taxed; and
3. combined duties: composed from these two categories of customs duties.

In special cases, to reinforce or replace customs duties, the following duties can be temporarily used:

- special customs duties: when imported goods are harmful to national manufacturers of the same goods;

- anti-dumping duties: when goods are imported at a much lower price than they are sold at in the exporting country; and
- balancing duties: when imported goods cause the slowing or stopping of the production of the same goods in Albania.

Other excise duties

The excise duty on excise goods subject to the provisions of the Custom Tariff Law is due to be paid when they are imported into or produced in the Republic of Albania.

The categories of goods subject to excise duty in Albania include:

- coffee;
- fruit juices, water and beverages;
- beer, wine, alcohol and alcoholic drinks;
- tobacco and its by-products;
- oil by-products; and
- cosmetic items, perfumes and toilet waters.

A full list of goods and the amount of excise duties are detailed in the annex of the Law on Excise Duties in the Republic of Albania (No. 8976, dated 12 December 2002). Article 12 stipulates that the tax authorities may exempt certain transactions from excise duties.

Under certain conditions, goods may be exempted from excise duties. Guideline No. 23, dated 7 August 2008, sets forth the procedures for exempting from excise duties the supply of gas and oil to fishing boats. Decree No. 25, dated 2 May 2008, provides for another exception: fuels used for the construction of power plants which would produce electric energy with a capacity of at least 5MW per source, as well as for its domestic sale will incur only 20 per cent of the excise duty that would otherwise be applicable. Consequently, 80 per cent of the excise duties will be exempted.

Value-added tax

The majority of goods and services are subject to VAT at a standard rate of 20 per cent, although certain exemptions apply (such as for financial services, postal services, non-profit organization supplies, drug and medicinal supplies, packaging and materials used in their production, supplies of electronic and written media for advertising, supplies of services at casinos and hippodromes (race tracks), sales of newspapers, magazines and advertisement services in them, as well as certain hydrocarbon operations).

VAT is applied at the rate of 0 per cent for the export of goods from the territory of the Republic of Albania and for the supply of services conducted outside the territory of the Republic of Albania by a taxpayer whose place of business, or whose residence in the case of an individual, is in Albania.

VAT is assessed, applied and paid on the import of goods as if the value-added tax were a customs duty. For machinery and equipment, imported for investment in production, construction industry and telecommunication, a VAT deferral payment system is applied. Article 26, Paragraph 2.1 of the VAT Law (No. 7928, dated 27 April 1995) stipulates conditions under which taxable persons are not liable to pay VAT on imported machinery and equipment used for performing their economic activity. While previously the law allowed for a deferral of VAT payment up to six months, the new Instruction on VAT (No. 17, dated 13 May 2008) has extended the deferral up to a period of 12 months. This period might, however, be lower under certain conditions, such as sale of the machinery to third persons.

The minister of finance has the right to extend this VAT deferral period for more than 12 months in cases where the cycle of the investment and the initiation of production, as well as rendering the services, are longer than 12 months.

VAT may be exempted from imported goods if those goods qualify under a temporary permit regime or transit regime as defined by the Customs Code of the Republic of Albania (Law No. 8449, dated 27 January 1999).

The taxpayer has the right to request VAT reimbursement if the entity has carried forward an amount of tax credit for three successive months, and the claimed reimbursement exceeds 400,000 Albanian leke (ALL; approximately €3,250 at the exchange rate of 123 ALL/euro). Reimbursement is also dependent on ranges of amounts that are claimed to be reimbursed. Exporters have the right to reimbursement if the value of transactions made in one month constitutes more than 50 per cent of the total value of sales including exports, and the excess amounts to ALL 400,000.

Local authority taxes

Local taxes are taxes levied, collected and administered by municipalities and communes.

Local taxes include:

- tax on immovable property, which consists of tax on buildings and tax on agricultural land;
- tax on accommodation at a hotel;
- tax on infrastructure effect (damages) of new constructions;
- tax on immovable property transfer right;
- tax on yearly registration of vehicles;
- charge on occupying a public place in the market;
- tax on boards (tables) displaying the names of business activities; and
- temporary fees.

Remittances to foreign recipients

This section includes a brief overview of the rules applicable to remittances of:

- dividends, royalty payments and consultancy services;
- import of goods;
- repatriation of capital;
- netting; and
- other remittances

by foreign businesses and investors operating in Albania.

Dividends, royalty payments, and consultancy services

According to Article 7 of the Law on Foreign Investments (No. 7764, dated 2 November 1993), income generated from dividends, royalty payments and consultancy services can be transferred outside the territory of Albania without the need to obtain any specific approval.

Foreign investors have the right to make such transfers in available currencies that are converted using the spot exchange rate on the day of the transfer transaction.

The Republic of Albania can restrict the right to transfer by applying relevant laws, including those related to tax payments and in compliance with court decisions and fulfilment of obligations.

Meanwhile, according to Article 13 of the Foreign Investment Law, if the amount of foreign currency funds to be transferred abroad is sufficiently large and will negatively impact Albania's balance of payments abroad, the Bank of Albania reserves the right to break down the entire amount into smaller amounts that will be transferred in parts and at different times.

Importation of goods

Payments in connection with the importation of goods and services in the ordinary course of business are generally permissible and can be undertaken freely through the filing of required documents directly with the authorized dealer/banker.

Repatriation of capital

Foreign capital invested in Albania is generally allowed to be repatriated, along with capital appreciation, if any, after the payment of taxes due on them. Generally, the repatriation of capital may take place upon:

- the winding-up of the company in Albania; and
- the sale of shares in the company to a third party.

The new Law on the Prevention of Money Laundering and Financing of Terrorist Activities (No. 9917, dated 19 May 2008), sets forth more stringent restrictions by requiring identification and proper reporting for amounts above ALL 1.5 million. The law requires banks to request from all entities making a transfer of a payment of ALL 1.5 million, or the equivalent amount in other denominations, to register and properly document the transaction in order to have transparency of the source and destination of the amount.

Netting

The Law on Accounting and Financial Statements (No. 9228, dated 29 April 2004) stipulates that the compensation of an asset against a liability and income against expenses is not permitted, unless it is permitted by an accounting standard.

National Accounting Standard No. 2, enforceable as of 1 January 2008, stipulates that assets are compensated against liabilities if the company has a legal right to net them off and can also use this right to do so.

Other remittances

No prior approval is required for remitting profits earned by Albanian branches of companies incorporated outside Albania to their head offices outside Albania.

Remittances of proceeds resulting from the whole or partial sale or winding-up of a foreign investment in Albania are permitted.

3.3

Income Tax and Social Contributions

Deloitte, Albania

This chapter explains personal income tax obligations and exemptions, as well as payments made as social contributions under Albanian law.

Personal income tax

Personal income tax is assessed upon the net income of individuals.

Personal income is taxed in Albania in accordance with the provisions of the Income Tax Law (No. 8438, dated 28 December 1998). The ministry of finance (Department of Revenue) through the General Taxation Department—an apex tax authority—implements and administers direct tax laws.

The Income Tax Law provides the general principle, according to which individual residents, during the tax period, are subject to personal income tax on all sources of income (inside and outside Albania), while non-resident individuals are only subject to personal income tax on sources of income generated in Albania.

Taxable income

For the purpose of determining the personal income tax, taxable income comprises:

- wages, salaries and other compensations derived from labour relations;
- income generated from profits of a partner or a shareholder in a commercial company;
- interest generated from bank deposits or interest generated from securities, excluding interest generated from government treasury bills or other securities issued before the effective date of this law;
- income derived from copyrights and royalties;
- income from emphyteusis, loans and leasing, excluding cases when income is generated from commercial activity, pursuant to commercial legislation;

- income generated from selling real estate;
- income of individuals generated from games of chance and casinos;
- income realized from the difference between the sales price and purchase price of the quotas and shares that a partner or shareholder possesses and sells to another person;
- other income that is not captured under the forms listed in this list, realized by resident or non-resident individuals, but has its source in the Republic of Albania.

Exempted income

The following income is exempted from personal income tax:

- income generated as a result of insurance under the obligatory social and health insurance scheme, as well as economic benefits for individuals with low or no income, as set out in the relevant legislation in force;
- fellowships of pupils and students;
- benefits received in the cases of disease and other hardship in accordance with the relevant legal provisions in force;
- benefits, both monetary and in kind, given as a bonus to owners of property for expropriation by the state for public interests;
- income exempted on the basis of international agreements ratified by the Albanian parliament.

Tax rates

Wages, salaries and compensations relating to actual employment shall be taxed according to rates illustrated in Table 1.

Dividends, income generated as the partner's profit, even if a single partner, interest from loans, deposits or similar contracts, income from copyright or intellectual property, as well as all other services or income that are not otherwise set out in other provisions of the law, shall be taxed at 10 per cent.

Table 1. Tax rates for wages, salaries and compensations

Minimum	Maximum	Rate (%)
0	10,000	0%
10,000+	30,000	+ 10% of the amount over ALL* 10,000
30,000+	more	10% of the amount over ALL 0

Note: ALL—Albanian leke

Payment procedures and penalties

All employers are required to withhold personal income tax from payments made in the form of wages of compensation according to the applicable rate, and are required to submit the tax to the tax authorities not later than the 20th day of the subsequent month of the transaction. If the procedures are not properly followed, there are a range of penalties available to the tax authorities which can be imposed upon non-complying employers, including:

- Failure of taxpayer to register or to update the information is liable to a fine of 25,000 Albanian leke (ALL) for each violation.
- Failure of taxpayer to submit the tax declaration within the required time period is liable to a fine of ALL 10,000.
- If tax liabilities are not paid by the 20th day of the next month, those responsible shall pay late interest payments in accordance with the Law on Tax Procedures (No. 9920, dated 19 May 2008), which also governs procedures for appealing and execution of administrative measures.
  - According to Article 114, the penalty amounts to 5 per cent of the unpaid tax liability for each month or prorated to the applicable portion of the month, after the due date of the declaration. The penalty can be no lower than ALL 10,000 and no higher than 25 per cent of the total unpaid tax liability.
  - In addition to the penalty, Article 76 stipulates that the late interest fee will be charged at 120 per cent of the monthly average of the last three months' inter-banking interest rate published by Bank of Albania.
- If payments made are not properly documented, taxes are not properly assessed and withheld, or information on income paid is hidden or falsified and thus insufficient funds are transferred to the state budget, those responsible shall pay the amount of tax liability and a fine equal to the amount of the tax liability.
- If proper records of taxpayers' income payments and taxes withheld are not maintained, including maintaining records of each taxpayer, those responsible are liable to pay a fine equal to ALL 10,000 for each violation.
- If any personal income tax due is under-declared, the employer must pay a penalty of 100 per cent of the unpaid amount of liabilities.
- If personal income tax of employees is withheld but not paid to the tax authorities, the employer must pay a penalty of 100 per cent of the unpaid amount of contributions. When such contributions are not paid to the tax authorities even after a period of three months from the due date set out in the relevant law, the employer is prosecuted.

Social and health contributions

Social and health contributions are payable by both the employer and employee based on the employee's monthly salary. The total social security contribution is 32.9 per cent of the monthly secured compensation salary. The minimum monthly secured compensation is ALL 14,830 (approximately €123) and the maximum monthly secured compensation is ALL 74,150 (approximately €613). The employer pays 21.7 per cent and the employee pays 11.2 per cent of the monthly secured compensation. The minimum monthly wage has been increased twice in 2008—first to ALL 16,000 from 1 January to 30 June 2008, and now to ALL 17,000 effective from 1 July 2008. As the minimum monthly wage is higher than the minimum monthly secured compensation, this has resulted in a new lower limit used to calculate social security contributions. Benefits that the individual receives are calculated as a portion of the average of the secured salary applicable to the last several months or years, depending on the type of benefit (eg. maternity leave, accident at work, etc.).

Contributions (from both the employee and employer) are calculated for each individual employee.

Declarations

Social security contributions must be made using the required declarations on a standard form and schedules provided by the tax authority:

- declaration of social and health insurance contribution payments;
- social and health insurance payrolls and employment-related income tax declaration payments;
- schedule of contributions due and employment-related income tax; and
- schedule of joiners and leavers.

Submissions, payments and penalties

Legal and physical persons registered for VAT purposes are obliged to make the relevant payments and declarations by the 20th day of the next month at a bank or post office, as well as submit a payroll list to the local tax office in the format prescribed by the tax authorities. There are measures in place which the tax authorities can utilize in the event of non-compliance:

- If a declaration is submitted late, or payment made late, an employer shall be liable to a penalty amounting to 5 per cent of the unpaid contribution liability for each month or prorated to the applicable portion of the month, after the due date of the declaration. The penalty can be no lower than ALL 10,000 and no higher than 25 per cent of the total unpaid tax liability. In addition to the penalty, a late interest fee is charged at 120 per cent of the monthly average of the last three months' inter-banking interest rate published by Bank of Albania (Law on Tax Procedures).
- If an employer has not declared each employee within 48 hours after the start of employment, such employer is liable to pay the mandatory contribution, as well as a penalty ranging between ALL 10,000 and ALL 20,000 for each violation.

- If the contributions are under-declared, an employer shall be liable to a penalty of 50 per cent of the contributions not declared.
- If contributions are withheld from an employee's wages, but are not paid over to the tax authority, an employer shall be liable to a penalty of 50 per cent of the unpaid amount of contributions. When these contributions are not paid to the tax authority even after three months from the date established in the law, then legal action is taken against the employer.

3.4

Accounting and Audit

Deloitte, Albania

The last few years have seen many developments relating to financial reporting in Albania, which in turn influence the auditing profession. The issues of transparency, accounting practices and corporate governance have become high agenda items in organizations worldwide.

During this period, a new law on accounting, a new law on banks and several other regulations have been approved, which impact on accounting in Albania. Until now, the only entities that had prepared financial statements in compliance with International Financial Reporting Standards (IFRS) were those that were subsidiaries of foreign entities, or those entities (either private or state-owned) that had received major loans or were being privatized (or were the subject of a takeover). The lack of an operational and active stock exchange in Albania had limited to a certain extent the need for IFRS financial statements.

However, the new law now requires implementation of IFRS by:

- all companies listed in the stock exchange and their subsidiaries subject to consolidation process;
- all second-level banks, financial institutions similar to banks, insurance and reinsurance companies, investment funds and other companies that have a licence to invest in bonds, even if they are not listed on the stock exchange;
- other companies not listed on the stock exchange that exceed in the previous two years the following two criteria:
  - annual revenue of 1,250,000,000 Albanian leke (ALL; approximately €10,050,000);
  - average number of employees of 100 per year.

Implementation of IFRS will not be without difficulties, due to the need to train both the accounting and financial personnel of companies, as well as local auditors. Professional organizations of accountants, especially the Institute of Authorized Chartered Auditors of Albania (IEKA) and the National Accounting Council have taken steps to fill this training gap. But, until now, only member firms of international audit and accounting firms have the proven skills to deal with IFRS, and these firms are few in Albania.

Legislative basis for accounting and audit

Chartered accountants in Albania are regulated by the Institute of Authorized Chartered Auditors of Albania (IEKA). The IEKA's activities are regulated by the Council of Ministers' Decision No. 150, dated 31 March 2000, which approved the rules for the organization of the approved chartered auditor profession. There are two other independent professional organizations of auditors and accountants, but the IEKA is the only one that has the power to legally supervise the profession. The IEKA is an associate member of the International Federation of Accountants (IFAC).

The Law on Accounting, which dates back to 1993, was accompanied by a General Accounting Plan, which was basically a chart of accounts, with detailed account numbers and rules. This chart of accounts was to be used by all Albanian companies. This law was replaced by the Law on Accounting and Financial Statements (No. 9228, dated 29 April 2004), in which Article 4 provides for the introduction of National Accounting Standards (NAS) and International Financial Reporting Standards (IFRS) from 1 January 2008. The new law requires specific entities to prepare accounts according to IFRS, while other companies will adopt the new NAS. The NAS is quite similar to the IFRS, but there are fewer standards under the NAS. In addition, individual standards included within the NAS and IFRS, although addressing the same topic, have some differences (eg. on cash flow statements).

Following the 2004 Law on Accounting and Financial Statements, the Council of Ministers issued a Decision No. 783, dated 22 November 2006, on the definition of accounting standards and rules preceding the introduction of the NAS.

The 2004 Law on Accounting and Financial Statements provides for the creation of the National Accounting Council (NAC) as an independent professional public organization. According to this law, the key tasks of the NAC are:

- to compile accounting standards;
- to compile an accounting system, which includes accounting rules, chart of accounts and financial statements format;
- to identify needs and propose solutions for improvements in accounting; and
- to give interpretations related to issues arising from practical use of accounting standards.

The new Albanian accounting standards empowered by the law have been published and entered into force on 1 January 2008.

Classification criteria

There are four main categories of commercial entities defined in the Law on Commercial Companies:

- collective entities;
- commandite entities (ie. entities where the liability of a minimum of one shareholder is limited up to his/her capital contribution and the liability of any other shareholders is unlimited);
- limited liability companies; and
- shareholding companies.

The last two categories of companies are the most common, and will be the focus of the new accounting requirements.

- Limited liability companies (ShPK) are established by one (in the case of sole traders) or several shareholders who are responsible for losses only up to the limit of the value of their contribution to the minimum capital required. Minimum capital requirements are ALL 100,000 (€833).
- Shareholding companies (ShA) are established by shareholders who are liable only up to the limit of their contribution to the starting capital. ShA companies comprise two main types: listed and unlisted. Minimum capital requirements are ALL 2 million (€16,666) for companies with private offers and ALL 10 million (€83,333) for companies with public offers.

Application of IAS/IFRS standards

The 2004 Law on Accounting and Financial Statements is part of a larger coordinated effort by the Albanian government to put its legislation in line with European Union legislation, and in general with international standards. Although Albania does not have an active stock exchange, which would be a key motivation to adopt IFRS, several transactions are taking place that require the companies involved to prepare financial statements based on IFRS. These transactions include strategic partnerships, acquisitions or applications for credit financing from international lending organizations such as the World Bank, European Bank for Reconstruction and Development, privatizations, etc. The new law stipulates the application of IFRS by "public interest entities". It is expected that by the end of 2008, financial services companies such as banks and insurance companies will start preparing financial statements in accordance with IFRS (although many of them are already preparing IFRS financial statements). However, the adoption of IFRS was not an easy process, as indicated by the delay in the law entering into force from 2006 to 2008.

Still, 2008, or rather 2009 (the year when the first annual IFRS accounting statements for the year 2008 will be submitted) will reveal the difficulties or ease with which the law is put into practice.

Financial statements

Under the 2004 Law on Accounting and Financial Statements, financial statements must include a balance sheet, a statement of profit and loss, a statement of changes in equity, a cash flow statement and explanatory notes which form part thereof, issued for the use of various stakeholders, governments, their agencies and the public.

The accounting year runs from 1 January to 31 December. Accounts must be submitted by 31 March.

Audit requirements

Following the rules of the previous Law on Commercial Entities, only Albanian companies which have a turnover of more than ALL 8 million (approximately (€65,000) were required to submit audited financial statements to the National Registration Centre by 31 March of the next reporting year. However, the new law now requires all entities registered with the National Registration Centre to submit financial statements and an auditor's report.

The financial statements must be audited by a certified auditor (member of IEKA), although the Bank of Albania and the Financial Supervisory Authority (responsible for insurance and pension companies) have strongly encouraged entities under their supervision to appoint internationally recognized audit firms as their auditors.

The standards that are being used by Albanian local auditors are the International Standards on Auditing (ISA), although there are many concerns about the application of these standards by local auditors, such as independence and quality control issues, due in part to the fact that most local auditors are sole practitioners.

3.5

Banking Sector

Raiffeisen Bank, Albania

Introduction

The Albanian banking sector has gone through significant change in the last 10 years. There are now 17 banks operating in a country with a population of just 3.2 million, of which nearly 35 per cent are under 20 years of age. The sector's total assets have increased from €3 billion in 2003, to over €6.8 billion by the end of 2008. This corresponds to 78 per cent of GDP.

Economic and political stability have created an environment for growth. In 2005, the mandatory payment of public sector employee salaries into the banks was a key initiative that increased the use of banking facilities and also enabled banks to lend with greater confidence and mitigated risk. The private sector has now followed suit.

A positive indication of the improving banking sector and its future potential is the recent entry into the market by IMI San Paolo and Société Générale through the acquisition of two local banks. This followed the 2004 acquisition of Albania's largest bank, the state owned Savings Bank, by Raiffeisen International, part of the Austrian banking group RZB.

History of the Albanian banking sector

The Communist regime nationalized all banking and financial institutions in 1945, and established the Bank of the Albanian State (now simply the Bank of Albania), which became the bank of issue. The bank also controlled foreign transactions, helped prepare financial plans for the economy, accepted savings deposits, financed economic activities and performed other banking functions. An agricultural bank was created in 1970 to provide credit facilities for agricultural cooperatives. On 10 August 1949, the Directorate of Savings was established to grant loans and to accept savings deposits in branches throughout the country; the system has grown steadily ever since.

When the Soviet Union collapsed in 1991, Albania decided to develop a market economy. The banking system changed to meet the demands of a free-market economy. In October 1996, the Islamic Conference's financing arm, the Islamic Development Bank, made a $12 million loan to Albania. However, the logic of the government's Islamic focus is unclear.

During the 1990s, the informal financial market absorbed millions of dollars of savings and remittances (estimates run as high as $1 billion), at the expense of the country's inefficient and uncompetitive banking sector. These pyramid investment schemes attracted hundreds of thousands of depositors—local estimates put participation in the companies at about 75 per cent of all households—by guaranteeing to pay high interest rates on cash deposits within a short period of time.

In 1997, the government's position was weakened considerably as a result of the collapse of four of the country's major pyramid investment schemes, leading to anarchic, nationwide demonstrations by furious investors. In January 1997, a 20,000-strong crowd marched through the capital, where it demanded that the government guarantee all deposits in these companies.

Much of the blame for the crisis rested with the government, whose policy towards the companies was not simply cavalier but actively encouraging. It did not pay attention to requests made by the central bank governor to regulate the pyramid schemes more tightly.

The privatization of the three state-owned commercial banks had long been advocated by the International Monetary Fund (IMF) and the World Bank, and in 2000 the government privatized the Rural Commercial Bank and the National Commercial Bank.

In April 2004, the state-owned Savings Bank of Albania was sold for $126 million to Raiffeisen International, part of the Austrian RZB Banking Group. The Savings Bank had 60 per cent market share of deposits and was by far the largest branch network in the country with 84 branches.

Legal framework

The banking system in the Republic of Albania has a two-tier structure. The first tier includes the Bank of Albania, whereas the second tier consists of banks and branches of foreign banks and non-bank financial subjects licensed by the Bank of Albania.

The Central Bank's activity is conducted in compliance with the Law on the Bank of Albania. The second tier banking system activity is conducted in compliance with the Law on Banks in the Republic of Albania:

- The Law on the Bank of Albania includes provisions providing for the Central Bank's powers and its activities, legal independence and the needs of a central bank to achieve its objectives as defined in the law.
- The Law on Banks in the Republic of Albania defines the core principles of banking activity in the Republic of Albania, and the main procedures and rules of licensing and supervision in the Albanian banking system.

Bank of Albania Supervisory Council

The Supervisory Council is charged with the overall direction and supervision of the policies, administration and operations of the Bank of Albania. In carrying out its functions, the Supervisory Council must periodically assess the economic situation, including the monetary, credit and exchange rate policies. Its functions and duties, as well as its composition, are set forth in the Law on the Bank of Albania.

Banking in Albania today

Banking sector developments over recent years have been impressive and dramatic. The banking network of branches has increased considerably from 188 in 2004, to 457 by the end of 2008, resulting in an expanding banking business and growth in the volume of assets and deposits. At the end of 2007, the banking system had good liquidity and capitalization figures. The sector was very profitable, ending with much improved figures compared to 2005. The rates of crediting to the economy were considerable, while the quality of the loans' portfolio remains at satisfactory levels.

Table 1. Banking sector performance (2006–2008)

Indicators	November '08	November '07	December '06
Capital adequacy (%)	17.5	17.5	18.10
Shareholder capital (€ million)	411	411	340
Net income (€ million)	75	79	60
Annual growth of loans' portfolio (%)	43.4	39.0	55.0

In order to provide a well-capitalized and balanced banking market and to push banks to carry out a more prudent control of business risks, at the end of 2006 the Bank of Albania adopted some regulatory amendments, which focused on lending activity. These amendments aimed to control the rate of growth and to enhance banks' transparency to clients. Based on the provisions in the new Law on Banks in the Republic of Albania, and in close cooperation with the commercial banks, the Bank of Albania introduced a Credit Registry in January 2008. This enabled banks to lend to all sectors with greater confidence and reduced risk.

Table 2. Ranking banks in Albania in terms of assets

	Banks	Total assets (€ million)	No. of branches	No. of personnel	No. of ATMs
1	Raiffeisen Bank Albania	2,047	100	1,373	178
2	Intesa San Paolo Albania	892	30	400	58
3	National Commercial Bank	842	40	519	50
4	Tirana Bank	662	44	387	63
5	Alpha Bank Albania	561	37	180	45
6	National Bank of Greece	235	30	250	17
7	Credins Bank	341	31	270	31
8	Société Générale Albania	288	40	300	26
9	Procredit Bank	258	26	600	47
10	Emporiki Bank Albania	196	20	94	20
11	Union Bank	96	23	90	34
13	International Commercial Bank	44	5	54	
12	United Bank of Albania	40	5	56	
14	Italian Development Bank	33	6	27	5
15	First Investment Bank	28	10	90	24
16	Credit Bank of Albania	17	2	31	

Source: AAB, September 2008

3.6

Insurance Market

Raiffeisen Bank, Albania

Overview of Albanian insurance market

The Albanian insurance market has been through significant changes in recent years. The modern insurance industry actually started in 1999, when the monopoly on the insurance market was dismantled by the government and a free market was created. In 2003, five insurance companies were active and today there are 10 insurance companies operating. Out of these 10 insurance companies, eight offer non-life insurance only, and two offer life policies solely.

From 2002 to 2005 Albanian insurance companies increased their premiums by an average of 4.3 per cent each year but the Albanian insurance market reached a turning point in 2006, reaching a premium growth of 12 per cent, compared to 2005 and has leapt forward again with gross written premiums increasing by 21 per cent in 2008 (January to November as compared with 2007—source Financial Services Authority). The premium structure has improved in the past years although a major share of the premium is still accounted for by car insurance, which is compulsory. In 2008 (January–November), when an annual premium of €48.5 million was recorded, the contribution of non-life insurance was €45 million, of which motor insurance constituted 62.8 per cent. The life market is growing, driven by the banks actively selling loan related life insurance and premium income increased by 31.7 per cent in 2008 versus 2007.

Insurance market players

During the period of the Albanian monopoly of the insurance market, INSIG held the dominant position. Today, INSIG is the fourth largest insurer in Albania with an overall market share of 17.2 per cent. The previously state-owned company is one of three Albanian insurers that offer both life and non-life products. Currently, the company is going through privatization, which is expected to finish soon.

SIGAL is by far the largest player in the market. With an overall market share of nearly 32 per cent, the company dominates the life market as well as the non-life segment. SICRED, a specialized life insurer, is the third player in this promising market of great potential. An overall market share of 17.9 per cent belongs to the number two position of SIGMA.

Table 1. Gross premium volumes, no. of contracts for the period January–June 2006–2008

In '000 ALL	January–November 2008	January–November 2007	Comparison 2008–2007
Gross premium volumes Non-life activity	6,535 mio 92.88% (as pct of Gross premium volumes)	5,409 mio	20.82%
Life activity	7.12% (as pct of Gross premium volumes)		
Gross premium no. of contracts Non-life activity Life activity	631,206	496,895	27.03%

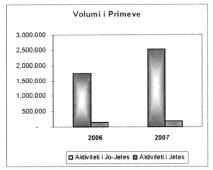

Figure 1. Gross premium volumes for the period January–June 2006, 2007

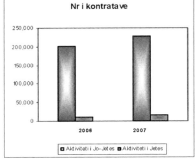

Figure 2. Number of contracts for the period January–June 2006, 2007

Table 2. Premium volumes in mandatory insurance and voluntary insurance, 2001–2006 and January–June 2006, 2007

Period	Mandatory insurance	Voluntary insurance	Total '000 ALL
2001	2,078,500	888,500	2,967,000
2002	2,675,090	1,128,650	3,803,740
2003	2,865,330	889,750	3,755,080
2004	2,968,040	1,183,390	4,151,430
2005	2,585,843	1,440,186	4,026,029
2006	2,976,912	1,530,242	4,507,154
January–June 2006	1,194,475	712,137	1,906,611
January–June 2007	1,827,573	888,940	2,716,513

Foreign investment

Due to the break-up of the monopoly in the Albanian insurance market, many foreign investors are trying to enter the market, attracted by the fact that domestic enterprises also operate in the markets of Macedonia and Kosovo. Albanian legislation is very similar to that of Kosovo and Macedonia. Many people in these countries share a common language; thus it is quite natural that Albanian insurance companies operate in these markets as well.

In 2004, foreign investors started to invest in Albania, when the International Finance Corporation (IFC) and European Bank for Reconstruction and Development (EBRD) purchased 39 per cent of the insurer INSIG from the state. In 2007, the two leading Austrian insurance companies, UNIQA and Vienna Insurance Group (VIG), began to cooperate with Albanian insurers as well: UNIQA is to cooperate with market leader SIGAL and VIG is to cooperate with SIGMA. UNIQA's cooperation is of particular interest, because SIGAL is—as mentioned—the Albanian market leader; additionally UNIQA cooperates with Raiffeisen Bank in central and Eastern Europe. As Raiffeisen Bank is by far the biggest bank in Albania, the insurance market is likely to be influenced by this partnership. UNIQA has an option that allows them to acquire the majority of SIGAL by the end of 2010.

The supervisory system in Albania

Legislation in the Albanian insurance sector is sufficiently well developed, and many changes are expected in the next few years. Since October 2006, the supervision of insurance and security companies, as well as pension funds, is in the hands of the Financial Services Authority (FSA).

Future changes in legislation will focus on stability, growth and adjustment to European Union (EU) guidelines. As a first step, the minimum capital required will be increased to €3 million in April 2008 (until now it has been €0.8 million). From January 2008, insurers have to apply IFRS rules in their reporting. Currently, the regulations for accruals, damage payment, solvency, record of financial results and re-insurance activity are being revised.

The objective of the FSA is to establish a professional supervisory system in the Albanian insurance market. Therefore improvements must be made on all levels. Specific attention will be paid to communication, electronic data analysis and early warning.

Finally, the FSA is trying to promote the availability and affordability of insurance among the domestic Albanian market.

A look into the future

The Albanian insurance industry has huge potential. However, for growth to flourish, the industry's "wild west" aspects must be tamed in order to create a level playing field for the market. Future development will be aided and supported by good and sustainable economic growth, and the planned improvements in the supervision system will ensure fair competition.

The insurance penetration is currently really low, 0.5 per cent of GDP only; an "average Albanian" pays approximately €10 per annum to any of the nine local insurance companies. As a result, Albanians are among the least insured people in Europe, a fact that offers plenty of scope for the insurance business to expand. As a result, insurance companies are actively introducing new products for private and business customers.

The national pension and medical insurance market will undergo reform in the future with the private sector as the only realistic solution. Albania suffers from natural disasters, such as earthquakes and flooding, and the need to develop a protection system is a high priority for the Albanian government. European companies have been invited to bring their know-how to the table for this initiative.

Conclusion

The Albanian economy is growing constantly and the same is true for the insurance market. An insurance penetration of 0.5 per cent of the GDP leaves huge room for improvement. Fair competition and stricter regulations, as well as the establishment of the Financial Services Authority, will make the insurance market more solid in the next few years.

In the past, the insurance sector has experienced harsh times, especially concerning minimum reserves. However, the government is beginning to understand that it must act, particularly in forcing all insurers to meet the new reserve standards and EU guidelines.

The prospects are promising; the non-life sector will remain the largest part of the market in Albania. Nevertheless, the life market has increased over the past years and once Albanians become aware of the role played by the insurance industry and their own need for safety it is likely to change and grow significantly.

3.7

Capital Markets

Raiffeisen Bank, Albania

Tirana Stock Exchange (TSE)

The Tirana Stock Exchange (TSE) was established on 2 May 1996. Listing on the TSE is organized on two levels, in accordance with quantitative and qualitative requirements stated in the listing rules of the TSE. Clearing and settlements are performed in cooperation with the Bank of Albania and second-tier commercial banks (Treasury Bills and Government Bonds), and the Albanian Shares Register (for joint-stock company shares). The TSE already has five members (three commercial banks and two private brokerage houses). Despite efforts made to attract domestic business to the capital market and continuous plans for the privatization of state-owned companies, no joint-stock company securities were listed on any of TSE trading levels as at January 2008.

Securities market

Government Treasury Bills and Treasury Bonds are the only debt instruments currently tradable on the domestic market in Albania. The Treasury Bills market was established in July 1994, and the first Treasury Bonds were issued in October 2002. In November 2006, the government issued the first five-year bonds. Two-year and three-year tenor bonds are a fixed-rate coupon whereas five-year bonds are floating rate. In December 2007, Albania invited bids for an auction of a new seven-year bond denominated in Albanian leke (ALL), worth ALL 6 billion, which also could be purchased in euros, in an effort to extend debt maturity.

Albania attained its first ever credit rating in June 2007 from Moody's Investors Service – "B1" with a stable outlook. This puts it four notches below investment grade.

Albania currently has an unfavourable debt maturity structure, but the government is taking further steps to extend the domestic public debt maturity and to strengthen its debt management.

Primary market

The only issuer of debt securities in Albania is the ministry of finance. The Bank of Albania performs the auctions on behalf of the ministry of finance. Government Treasury Bills are issued in local and foreign currency, while the bonds are issued in local currency only. The ministry of finance is planning to issue euro-denominated bonds.

Securities are settled on a T+2 basis. The minimum amount for participation in the Treasury Bill auction is ALL 300,000 (approximately €2,500); the minimum amount for bonds is ALL 1 million.

Private individuals, resident or non-resident, are allowed to participate directly in the primary Treasury Bill auctions or via licensed banks, while in Treasury Bond auctions foreign investors are allowed to participate directly if their bids are competitive, otherwise (for non-competitive bids), they are obliged to participate only through a licensed bank.

In July 2007 (a typical month), the local currency equivalent of €94 million was offered at auction.

Secondary market

The secondary market is not very liquid and is small in volume. Treasury Bills are mostly traded between banks and individuals in the retail market. Starting from November 2006, Treasury Bonds became more easily tradable between banks, corporate institutions and private individuals.

Non-residents can complete transactions on the secondary market through a licensed bank and by using an escrow account. Licences are issued by the Albanian Securities Commission. Private individuals are subject to 10 per cent tax on interest income.

Table 1. Local currency debt instruments' descriptions

DESCRIPTION *	Gov T-bills	Gov T-bonds
Issuer	Ministry of Finance	Ministry of Finance
Currency	Albanian lek (ALL)	Albanian lek
Minimum Denomination	ALL 0.3	ALL 50 mn
Tenor(s)	3, 6 and12 months	2, 3 and 5, 7 years
Interest Rate/Coupon	zero coupon (discount)	coupon
Coupon Payment Dates	none	semi/annual
Interest Accrual Basis	365 days	360 days
Day Count Basis	Actual/365	30/360
Amortization Schedule	Bullet	Bullet
Form of Issue	Book-Entry, Dematerialized	Book-Entry, Dematerialized
Total Outstanding at Face	ALL 237,450 mln (Market Value)	ALL 144,740 mln (Market Value)
PRIMARY MARKET		
Auction Style	Dutch Auction	English Auction
Agent	Central Bank of Albania	Central Bank of Albania
Average Issue Size	ALL 30,014 mln monthly	ALL 5,500 mln monthly
Frequency	3, 6 months monthly, 12 months biweekly	2Y-monthly; 3Y-quarterly; 5Y-quarterly; 7Y semiannual
Participation	via authorized dealers only	via authorized dealers only
Settlement	T+2	T+2
Reuters/Bloomberg Screens	Reuters: AL/TSY01; AL/TSYRESULT01	Reuters: AL/TSY03 - 05; AL/TSYRESULT02 - 04
SECONDARY MARKET		
Trading Floor(s)	Interbank	Interbank
Liquidity	poorly liquid	poorly liquid
Settlement	T+0	T+0
Average Trade Size		
Clearing Mechanism	Central Bank of Albania	Central Bank of Albania
Custody	Banks licensed from FSA	Banks licensed from FSA
Trading Hours	9am-2:30pm local time; London (-1h); New York (-5h)	
Reuters/Bloomberg Screens	Reuters: SSAL01-Raiffesien Bank; NCAT 02-National Commercial Bank; ABBT01-American Bank of Albania	
RETAIL MARKET		
Trading Floor(s)	OTC	OTC
Liquidity	30 mln daily turnover	n/a
Settlement	T+0	T+0
Average Trade Size	ALL 2.0 mln	n/a
Clearing Mechanism	Central Bank of Albania	Central Bank of Albania
Custody	Via Banks licensed by FSA	Via Banks licensed from FSA
Trading Hours	9am-2:30pm local time; London (-1h); New York (-5h)	
Reuters/Bloomberg Screens	Reuters: SSAL01-Raiffesien Bank; NCAT 02-National Commercial Bank; ABBT01-American Bank of Albania	
REGULATION/TAXES		
Restrictions on Foreign Investment	Non-residents have access since 1996. Direct access to primary auctions or via Banks licensed by FSA	Access for non-residents since 2007. Via Banks licensed by FSA
Income Tax (for retail)	10%	n/a
Income (Coupon) Tax	n/a	n/a
Capital Gains Tax *	10% - institutional, 10% - retail	

Source: ministry of finance; National Bank; Raiffeisen RESEARCH

Appendix

Appendix 1

Contributors' Contact Details

Deloitte Albania sh.p.k
Rr. "Murat Toptani"
Eurocol Center
Kati 8-te
Tirana
Albania
Tel: +355 4 22 77 950 or 929
Fax: +355 4 22 77 990
Email: nsokoli@deloittece.com and daconnolly@deloittece.com
Website: www.deloitte.com/al

Kalo & Associates
59 Kavaja Avenue
P.O.Box # 235
Tirana Tower, 5th Floor
Tirana
Albania
Tel: +355 4 233 532
Fax: +355 4 224 727
Email: info@kalo-attorneys.com
Website: www.kalo-attorneys.com

Ard Kelmendi
Email: ardkelmendi@gmail.com

Raiffeisen Bank Albania
European Trade Centre
Bulevardi Bajram Curri
Tirane
Albania
Tel: +355 4 275 510
Fax: +355 4 275 550
Email: robert.wright@raiffeisen.al
Website: www.raiffeisen.al

Index